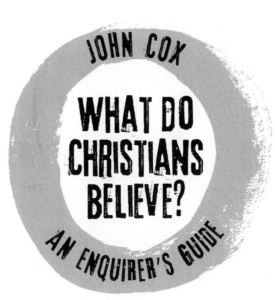

JOHN COX

WHAT DO CHRISTIANS BELIEVE?

AN ENQUIRER'S GUIDE

www.kevinmayhew.com

First published in Great Britain in 2014 by Kevin Mayhew Ltd
Buxhall, Stowmarket, Suffolk IP14 3BW
Tel: +44 (0) 1449 737978 Fax: +44 (0) 1449 737834
E-mail: info@kevinmayhew.com

www.kevinmayhew.com

9 8 7 6 5 4 3 2 1 0

ISBN 978 1 84867 702 9
Catalogue No. 1501428

Cover design by Rob Mortonson
© Images used under licence from Shutterstock Inc.
Edited by Nicki Copeland
Typeset by Richard Weaver

Printed and bound in Great Britain

Contents

About the author

Having been a parish priest in Prescot, Liverpool and Newtown, Birmingham, John Cox spent five years as a selection secretary at Church House Westminster. He was then Director of Ordinands and Post-ordination Training for the Diocese of Southwark, and Canon of Southwark Cathedral before returning to parish life at Holy Trinity, Roehampton. In 1995 he was made Archdeacon of Sudbury and on retirement in 2006 became Diocesan Director of Education in the Diocese of St Edmundsbury and Ipswich until a second retirement in 2010. He now spends his time as Chair of Governors of a primary academy, playing golf, travelling, and writing and editing for Kevin Mayhew.

Introduction

Approaching a minister, clergyman or priest can feel a little daunting for those who have never had anything to do with them. The impression of what they will be like often depends on what has been seen on TV or read about in the newspapers. Most clergy are, in fact, very ordinary people, neither 'holier than thou' nor wanting to thrust religion down your throat. But as adults, most of us first learn about what Christians do and believe through people other than the clergy. They talk about their faith, they suggest we go along with them to church, we are invited to a wedding, we attend a funeral. They will be delighted to welcome you to church. What is then experienced may be strange, confusing, uplifting, a pleasant surprise, or perhaps a little off-putting. But what if we want to learn more? We can, of course, ask someone we know who is a Christian; we could try going back to a church service; we could look it up on Google. There is no 'right' way; only the way that most helps you.

This book is one of those possible ways for you to learn more about what Christians believe and what they do. It does not treat you as a 'dummy', nor does it use a lot of technical terms. Where they are used they are explained. It attempts to 'de-mystify' Christianity – not because it takes away that essential sense of mystery that any talk about God and the things of faith will always have, but in the sense of not assuming that you already know a lot. It also seeks to talk in straightforward ways about the Bible, about God, about prayer and about what goes on in church.

The book acknowledges that if you want to go deeper then it will take some effort – in trying to understand the Bible, for example. If you want to learn to play the piano you know it will take some effort – but it's worth it. The journey of faith also takes effort – both to understand it better and, most of all, to live it. The

Christian claim is that the effort is infinitely worth it, and it isn't all up to us. There are other people to help and – most importantly – God will give us a hand too.

It is inevitable that, on occasions, specific content will reflect particular denominations. For example, not all congregations use formal worship from authorised books of services. Evangelical and Pentecostal churches are more likely to have informal, even spontaneous acts of worship that depend more upon the charismatic input of a worship leader than on any predetermined service pattern. Comments, therefore, about formal liturgical worship would not apply to the experience of such informal worship. Likewise the range of church buildings and buildings used by congregations varies enormously and certainly the medieval parish church will not be the norm for many churchgoers and enquirers. Where possible the book attempts to take this range of experience and provision into account and to cover as wide a variety of practice as is reasonably possible. My apologies for any omissions.

One other point of explanation is perhaps needed. The term Anglican refers to the church established at the Reformation as the Church of England and also includes those churches that have particular links to the Church of England through belief and practice, and who look to the Archbishop of Canterbury as their symbolic head. Together these churches form the Anglican Communion. The term Catholic has normally been used to refer to the Roman Catholic Church or a member of that Church. Within the Anglican tradition there are those who would also call themselves catholic. They are what is commonly called 'high church' or Anglo-Catholics. I have tried to make these distinctions clear where the meaning requires it.

A small book like this will not tell you everything but it will give you a start, a way in. May you enjoy the journey.

CHAPTER 1

What's in the Bible?

Between the covers

The Bible is sacred to Christians. They call it the Word of God, or the **Holy Scriptures**. It looks like a book, it can be bought in bookshops and it would not be out of place on a bookshelf. But in fact it is not simply a book – it is a whole collection of books bundled together between covers.

The word 'Bible' means 'books'. It is more like a mini library of books – around 66 different ones (on the actual number see below). They have different authors and were written over a period of many centuries. The final number of books included in the Christian Bible was not settled until about AD 400.

It is a 'library' of two halves: the **Old Testament** (39 books) and the **New Testament** (27 books). A testament is an 'agreement' or 'covenant' and refers to the relationship agreed by God first with his people the Jews and then to the followers of Jesus Christ. The Old Testament books were part of the Jewish Scriptures and were later adopted by the Christian Church. The New Testament books were then added to them. Broadly speaking, the Old Testament tells of the relationship of the Jewish people with God and the New Testament books reflect the life and teachings of Jesus and the experience of the early Christian Church.

The actual **number of books** that make up the Bible was long disputed, and disagreement continues. The Jewish Scriptures are divided into three main groups of books: the Torah (the Law), the Prophets and the Writings. They were written originally in Hebrew and then translated into Greek, and at that point additional books were added. It is these additional books, generally known as the

Apocrypha, that make the difference. The Roman Catholic Church accepts these books as part of the Holy Scriptures and they bring the number of Old Testament books up to 46, while Protestant churches accept only the books that were written in Hebrew.

The Old Testament

The **Old Testament**, written in Hebrew with some Aramaic texts and translated into Greek, was the version the early Christians knew. With the increasing influence of the Church of Rome, Latin **translations** were the norm in western Europe. While parts of the Bible were translated into English as early as the seventh century and the famous Lindisfarne Gospels have an English translation alongside the Latin text, it wasn't until the fourteenth century that John Wycliffe translated the whole of the Bible into English. The setting out of the Bible into chapters and verses did not appear until 1560, and the first authorised version in English appeared in 1611 – the King James Bible. These days there are dozens of different translations, from scholarly to popular – e.g. the New Revised Standard Version, the Jerome Bible, the Good News Bible, *The Message*. Parts of the Bible have been translated into more than 1300 different languages.

Within the broad three-fold division of the Old Testament that the Jews have traditionally used (see above), the first five books of the Bible are known as the **Pentateuch**. The word reflects the way the material was set out on five scrolls. They tell the story of God's choice of the Hebrew people and the Law he gave them by which to live good lives. It begins with the creation of the universe and of all living things, including men and women (the first of whom were named Adam and Eve). The emphasis is not that something was created out of nothing (that is a modern concept) but that out of chaos God created order. Adam and Eve were disobedient, and this resulted in a break-up of that harmonious order of the world and led eventually to a great flood that God sent as a punishment. Later, God called Abraham and there was a renewed relationship, and the rest of the Pentateuch tells the story first of Joseph and then of Moses when the Hebrew people escaped from slavery in Egypt and wandered in the wilderness for 40 years (the Exodus c.1250 BC). It was during that time that Moses was said to have received the Law from God.

Books like Samuel, Kings and Chronicles tell of the **History** of the Hebrew people once they had settled in Palestine and established a monarchy. Their most famous kings were David, who killed Goliath (c.1000 BC), and his son Solomon, who was known for his wisdom. As with many countries, the fortunes of Israel varied greatly – Solomon built up a considerable empire but interfamily strife and rivalry divided the nation (c.920 BC) and made them prey to other nations such as the Assyrians and Babylonians. Invasion resulted in exile, and even a return to their homeland never really restored their fortunes fully. Later it was the Greeks who ruled the Jews, and by the time of Jesus it was the Romans. Those who wrote down the history of the Hebrews saw these variations in fortune as a reflection of the people's relationship with God – obedience and faithfulness resulted in good fortune; worshipping foreign gods and disobedience resulted in disaster.

It was around and after the time of the Exile that the **Prophets** were prominent (eighth to sixth centuries BC) – men such as Isaiah, Jeremiah and Ezekiel as well as the so-called 'lesser prophets', such as Amos, Hosea, Micah and Joel. The prophets saw themselves as spokesmen for God, delivering messages of judgement on the wrongs of the nation – its injustice as well as its idolatry – or offering hope in times of difficulty. Prophets were 'forth-tellers' rather than foretellers – they read the signs of the times and interpreted them in the light of their faith and the way they believed God would act.

At the heart of Jewish national life was its worship. This was centred on the Temple at Jerusalem that Solomon had built. Much of the worship involved the sacrifice of animals or birds, both as a sign of repentance for wrongdoing and in thanksgiving to God. But there was also celebration, as when a king was crowned, and plenty of singing. The **Psalms** are a kind of hymn book for the Temple. Many of them are believed to have been composed by King David. They reflect a wide range of emotions: joy and grief, anger and thanksgiving, a sense of the closeness of God and also a sense of his absence. Today they still have an important place in Christian worship and spirituality.

Over many centuries, and influenced by the culture of neighbouring countries such as Egypt, there developed a tradition of wise men (sages) who reflected on the life of the people, and whose ideas were eventually collected together in such books as Proverbs, Job and Ecclesiastes. In general, the emphasis in the **Wisdom** movement is on everyday experience: in Proverbs, for example, there is virtually no mention of religion or God. The focus is on what makes for a reasonable, wise life.

The New Testament

The **New Testament** has four accounts of Jesus' life, known as **Gospels**. The word 'gospel' means 'good news'. As well as relating events in Jesus' life, they record what he taught. The major focus in each Gospel is on the last week of his life that led to his crucifixion and resurrection.

The **Acts of the Apostles** provides a picture of the life of the early Church as the Christian faith spread throughout the Mediterranean world. It focuses on major figures such as St Peter and St Paul.

The teaching of the early Church is contained in the **Epistles** – letters sent to Christian communities by St Paul and others to guide them in their understanding of what Jesus had done and how they should behave.

The final book of the Bible, and one of its strangest, is the **Book of Revelation**. It contains a series of visions setting out what will happen in the last days when the current order of the cosmos will come to an end and there will be a 'new heaven and a new earth'.

In scope, therefore, the Bible goes from the time when the universe came into existence through to the time when it will end. Within that scope it is a story of God's dealings with humanity, especially through the people of Israel and through the life and impact of Jesus of Nazareth.

CHAPTER 2

How to read the Bible
Breaking the code

A lot of people have been put off the Bible by starting at the beginning and trying to plough their way through. They open it at the book of Genesis and become entangled in a description of creation which, to many modern eyes, appears to be a piece of fantasy. It may be religious fantasy, but fantasy nonetheless. It just doesn't fit with a world where science tells us that the universe is billions of years old, it all began with a Big Bang and life certainly didn't appear on the third day. Yet they know that Christians hold the Bible to be very precious and call it the Word of God so therefore it must be true. So it is not only the Bible that feels weird – Christianity feels weird, and there's an end of the matter.

And that is a pity, because it means that such people have been put off from discovering what an exciting, beautiful, violent, consoling and challenging book the Bible can be.

What you make of the Bible is not just a matter of what the Bible might say to you, but also what you bring to the way you read it. If you read it as though it were a scientific text book or only as historical fact, you'll soon start feeling it's got things wrong. It isn't science and it isn't simple history. But that doesn't mean it hasn't important things to say and lessons to teach about what it is to be human, the way God relates to the world, and the spiritual nature of things. The story of Jonah, for example, is not supposed to be the accurate, historical account of a man who was actually swallowed by a whale and then spewed out again. It is a story about the way God works in spite of his servants not always doing what he wants them to do. It speaks of a God of forgiveness, even when we feel revengeful. And the whale adds a great piece of drama to the story.

The best way to begin reading the Bible is to see it as story. There is a lot more than story in the Bible: there are poems and legal codes, there are hymns and letters, there are accounts of God's dealings with nations and with individuals, there is spiritual teaching and there are visions of the future. But it's not a bad way to begin. Stories are among the most powerful ways of telling truths about what it is to be human, even if they are not historically or scientifically 'true'. The Hebrew people were more interested in story than they were in abstract ideas. If they wanted to talk about jealousy they told a story about two brothers, what happened when one became jealous of the other and how it ended in tragedy. Did it actually happen in the way it was told? That didn't matter too much – but the truth about what happens when jealousy gets hold of the human spirit is importantly true. If we want to get to grips with the Bible, we have to be clear that 'truth' and 'fact' are not necessarily the same thing – ask a poet, an artist, a lover or a saint.

When you read the Bible it is, of course, perfectly possible just to sit down, read it as it is and take it or leave it. It might puzzle you, cheer you up, confuse you, depress you or mystify you. It all depends on the passage and how you are feeling at the time. And there's nothing wrong with that. But if you want to go a bit deeper and try to understand what a passage means – what it's getting at – then you will have to do a bit of work.

Some work to do

Begin by asking yourself a few questions: When? Where? For whom? What? Why?

When was this written? If you want to be accurate you will probably need some help – perhaps from a book that gives some background to the Bible or to particular books of the Bible (a Bible commentary). Such books are always worth the investment. But even just reminding yourself that it was hundreds, if not thousands, of years ago will help you to realise that it will have a very different view on the way life is – no aeroplanes, no smartphones, no washing machines, no designer clothes. Travel and communication were more difficult. Much more time was spent on basic chores and just surviving. Luxuries were only for the very rich.

Was it written at the same time as the events it talks about? Usually not. Clearly, no one was producing an account of creation at the time it happened. And even events involving Jesus were not written down during his lifetime. It took 30, 40, 60 years even, before the Gospels were completed. But that doesn't mean they were just made up. There was a long and lively tradition of keeping stories alive and accurate without writing them down. It does mean, however, that the situation at the time of writing will have had some impact on the way the story of Jesus was written. Think of the difference an account of the Holocaust written 50 years after the event would be to one that was written at the time. Laws that were appropriate to a people who were changing from being nomadic to city dwellers, who lived when there were no antibiotics, no unions, no global bankers, were not intended for the modern world. That doesn't mean they might not still apply, but nor does it mean they will inevitably be appropriate today.

Where was it written? Was it written amidst a people who were city dwellers or farmers? To describe God as a shepherd, for example, as Psalm 23 does, is not likely to have been the way a city dweller would think about God. It's an image, a picture of God that made very good sense to country people who knew the care a shepherd had to take of his sheep – it's not a factual description of God. Was it written in Palestine or in the foreign country of Babylon? When the homeland of the Jews was conquered by the Babylonians, many of the people were transported to Babylon where they lived in exile. Life would have been very different in the safety of their own country to living in a foreign land where they had no rights, where they were outsiders, exiles.

For whom? Was it written for people who were from a Jewish background or a mainly Greek background. This made a difference to the way Matthew and Luke wrote their Gospels. If you were to write an account of the dramatic events of 9/11 you might want to put it a little differently if you were writing to an American than if you were writing to an Arab. The facts may be the same, but conveying the event effectively might require two different approaches. Were the people being addressed the people with power or were they ordinary folk; were they slaves or slave owners?

In our largely secular age we need to remind ourselves that the Bible comes from times when religion was the norm – everyone was religious. Talk of God was commonplace. That there was God or gods was just assumed. Only the fool said there was no god. We're in a different world today in western Europe; people have quite different mindsets. It was also a pre-scientific world, so explanations of many things in the natural world – e.g. storms, eclipses of the sun or earthquakes – weren't down to physics but to spirits and gods.

What sort of piece is this? Is it a story, a poem, a law, a love song, a piece of propaganda, a letter to a group or to an individual, a hymn or a genealogy? The Bible has all these, and more besides, and misunderstanding a hymn for a law would obviously confuse its meaning.

Most importantly, **Why** was it written? Was it written to convey scientific knowledge or truths about the human condition? Was it written to encourage a people who were in danger of losing all hope, or to remind them of God's demands on his people when they were in danger of forgetting him? Was it written just to tell a story about someone or, more importantly, to convey the significance of that person – Jesus, for example? Was it written to attack an enemy or to emphasise a viewpoint?

Most often the reason was either to tell us about what it is to be human and the possibilities and challenges that presents, or it was to tell us about God – what he is like, how he acts, what he expects. These things are important, for they feed not just the head but also the heart and the spirit.

When Christians say that the Bible is the **word** of God, they are careful not to say that it is the **words** of God. That's not just a quibble; it is important. The Bible is not a set of divine dictations for which the various authors acted like mechanical scribes. It is the product of human minds and spirits inspired by their belief in God and their relationship with God, living amidst a community of faith. Through these human words it is possible for God to 'speak' to us – the human words convey the word, the message, the communication of God. It's not mechanical and we can get it wrong, but being open to what is presented to us, trying our best to understand what it is seeking to say – not only to the people of its own time but to us now – that is the way the Bible is and becomes God's word for us.

Does the Bible ever contradict itself? Yes. Does it ever get things wrong? Yes. It is an authoritative book – that is, it can be relied upon in the overall consistent picture it gives of being human and in the picture it builds up about God. But it is not infallible. It can get dates wrong, it can muddle up names. But through its stories and its accounts, its poetry and its wise sayings, its teaching and its visionary hope it can inspire us, comfort us, challenge us and teach us.

So if you start at Genesis, approach the Bible as story with insights about the relationship between men and women, about the human condition and its relationship with God and with the world of nature. The stories are the result of much reflection on the way life is, could be and should be in the company of a creator, caring but demanding God. It is realistic about the frailty of the human condition and its fallibility, but it is also optimistic about the huge potential of the human spirit and the transforming power of a relationship with God. What it isn't is a scientific record of what happened when the world started and humankind first appeared on the scene.

Some suggestions for reading the Bible:

- Start with stories – either about Old Testament figures like Abraham, Joseph or David, or with stories about Jesus or St Paul.

- Have a look at the Psalms – they often reflect very ordinary feelings.

- Don't try too much in one go – it is much better to spend time reflecting on a short passage than to rush through several chapters.

- If there are bits that you find boring – such as lists of family names or endless laws – just skip them. You can always come back to them.

- Try to keep an open mind – just because something sounds strange, don't write it off. Read with the expectation that it has something to teach you, to sustain you, to guide you.

- Obtain a short, single-volume Bible commentary to help with some of the background.

- Give it a chance – stick at it. The meaning of the text is not always straightforward or obvious, so be prepared to do a bit of work.

- The Bible is an important book and deserves respect, but Christians don't worship a book; they worship God.

- Don't be afraid to ask questions. If something sounds strange – e.g. a miracle – ask what might have happened, but more importantly, think about what the account is trying to tell you.

- Some things are mysterious – but they are worth exploring even when we cannot fully explain them. Being in love is difficult to fully explain, but it's a great experience.

- Enjoy!

CHAPTER 3

What is prayer?

More than asking

'There are no atheists in foxholes' is a proverb that came out of the Second World War, although its exact origins are obscure. In situations of danger it seems natural to turn to God and ask for help. Even people who would not normally call themselves religious do it. When all other help seems inadequate, we turn to the divine, the supernatural.

But it is not only when we are in danger. We may be facing an exam or a job interview and we know our nerves are doing us no favours. We want help to do our best. We may be desperately tired and want a bit more strength to get through the job in hand. We may be short of money and need some cash badly. Our partner may have just left and we want them back. So we ask for help, for things we need, things that we think will turn our lives around. We ask God, sometimes as a first resort, more often when all else fails.

It is natural to think that prayer is about **asking**. As a call of desperation it might be quite short, wrung out of us. It will almost certainly have no idea how God might answer it; we just want him to do what we ask. We might not even be sure just who the god is we have called out to. But there are plenty of people who can tell us that God has answered such prayers – a cheque appeared unexpectedly in the post; they felt calmer than they expected in the interview and were offered the job; they survived in spite of the danger. But, of course, there are also those who did not receive what they wanted – a friend died in spite of prayers for him to recover; the bailiffs arrived, not a cheque; the nerves got the better of the job-seeker. Answered prayer may seem like a miracle, but unanswered prayer can be a problem.

We shouldn't think of God as a kind of super slot machine – mechanically delivering the goods when we insert the coin of our prayer. In the prayer that Jesus taught his friends – the Lord's Prayer – there is the phrase 'Your will be done, on earth as it is in heaven'.[1] Christians assume that what God wills, what he wants, is ultimately for our good, because he is a loving God. Just giving us what we want may not be for the best. Parents know that in dealing with the demands of their children. God loves us but he wants us to grow in freedom and in responsibility – and just doling out things, even good things, will not necessarily help us to do that.

We also have to learn to be loving towards one another, not just towards God, and that means acting with generosity towards others, to be forgiving and unselfish. On the big scene that means acting justly and peacefully. People don't always do that, and men, women and children are sometimes hurt as a result. And we live in a world where 'laws of nature' operate. If a brick falls on your head it is going to hurt, and perhaps worse. God won't interfere to stop it. If we see the brick coming we might call out to God, but the best thing is to duck!

Because we don't always get what we want, we can think God doesn't care, won't do the things we ask for, or just simply isn't there. We think that prayer doesn't work. But **prayer is much more than just asking for things**.

Prayer is also about such things as **thanks, wonder, praise, saying sorry, listening** and, most importantly, our **relationship with God**.

---

1. In the Gospel of Matthew, chapter 6, verse 10.

Thanks

Counting our blessings sounds very old-fashioned. But news headlines on almost any day give us reason to be thankful. We aren't starving, we aren't in the middle of a violent civil war, our family hasn't been wiped out in a hurricane. Life might not be easy, but if we take a moment or two to reflect, there is so much to be grateful for. There are the everyday things that we have because of the love, the work, the thoughtfulness of others. There are the excitement, the delight and the enjoyment we have through music, art, films and reading. There are the benefits of a world of resources – of food, energy and materials. For those who believe that everything originates in the creative love of God, thanks are due not only to people but also to God. Saying 'thank you' is part of prayer. Being thankful when everything is not going well is a sign of growing in spiritual maturity.

Wonder

To respond to the world around us with delight is a spiritual matter. A beautiful sunset, a dramatic waterfall, the song of a lark can raise the spirit and give us goosebumps. But so, too, can exceptional examples of human endeavour – a magnificent cathedral, a spectacular road system, a piece of art or an outstanding sporting achievement. We wonder at it. They are wonder-ful. If we allow time to let the experience wash over us and enter into our hearts, it enlarges our sense of being alive. When the experience of God does that to us, our response is a prayer of wonder, a prayer in which words aren't even needed.

Praise

We all like to be praised. And we all need to be praised. It builds up our sense of worth and our self-confidence. Never to be praised is very damaging. Of course, always to be looking for praise and to receive nothing but praise can be equally harmful.

So does God *need* praise? No, he doesn't. But praising God is something *we* need to do. Praising another person doesn't only boost them, it also enlarges us. We cannot praise others if we are only concerned about ourselves. We cannot praise others if we do not have a generosity of spirit about other people's achievements. In the act of praise we grow in those good attitudes that produce praise. That is why we need to praise – it's part of our spiritual growth. And praising God means we have taken the trouble to think about God, about all that is praiseworthy in what he does and what he is and are prepared to say so.

Saying sorry

We all get things wrong. It's not that we just make mistakes in the way we do things; we make mistakes in how we treat others. Making mistakes or failing at something are not the worst things in the world. What matters is what we do about the mistakes and the failings. Do we pretend they didn't happen? Do we hope no one will notice? Do we beat ourselves up about them? Or do we try to put things right, to make a better job of it next time? Do we ask forgiveness of others? Do we forgive ourselves? It's not always easy to do that. Saying sorry to God requires a lot of honesty and trust: honesty about ourselves and trust that God will forgive us – which he has promised to do. Confession (the posh word for saying sorry) isn't grovelling – it's being honest about the bits we get wrong, the bits we feel ashamed about. It's the start of making things better, of being better. It isn't a question of informing God – he already knows all about us – it is for our sake, so that we can grow in self-awareness and trust.

Listening

It's a mistake to think that prayer is all about us talking to God. It's also about silence and listening. In our modern world we seem to find silence difficult. Many students seem to need music plugged through their ears to be able to study. We can't travel happily in a lift without there being music. Silence can be disturbing. For one thing, it means we are left listening to our thoughts – and that can sometimes be uncomfortable. But if we want to become more fully human, we need to find time to listen – to listen to others, to listen to ourselves, to listen to God.

'Be still, and know that I am God!' says the psalmist (Psalm 46:10). He didn't only mean stop rushing around thinking you can do everything; he also meant being quiet, using silence to discover the presence of God and to listen to God.

Using silence as prayer takes practice. To start with, all you hear may be the thoughts that rush around in your head. Learning stillness and silence takes time – but the great saints all tell us of its value as a part of what it is to pray.

Relationship with God

Prayer is not a matter of completing a checklist – ticking the boxes marked Wonder, Praise, Sorry, etc. Prayer is more than the sum of the parts. Its purpose is **to grow in relationship with God**. All prayer arises from and expresses our relationship with God.

Christians believe that God loves us and that he longs for us to love him back. He invites us to be his lovers. And love is all about a relationship. For some people, their experience of first coming to know God is like falling in love – it is as exciting and as dramatic as that. For others, their relationship with God builds up gradually, perhaps over many years and with plenty of ups and downs. However a loving relationship begins, it needs working at, attention and commitment, and it will certainly change over the years. Prayer is a way of helping our relationship with God grow and develop. It opens us up to God and, though it may feel that prayer is our work, the truth is that in prayer God is at work – in us.

Alone and together

We can pray alone, and much of prayer is like that – in a quiet place on our own. It's a private matter, and being asked about how you pray can feel like an intrusion into something that is very personal, especially when you are first trying to pray. But a lot of prayer also takes place as part of worship with others – when people join together to say prayers as well as to sing and to listen to Bible readings and sermons. Public prayer like that is quite a different sort of experience – and there is a place for both private and public prayer.

We can sometimes feel that we don't know what to say in our prayers, and that is when the prayers of others or books of prayers can be useful. The 'Amen' we say at the end of prayer is like saying, 'Yes, I agree with that,' and when our own words feel inadequate, it can be helpful to be able to say 'Amen' to what others have said or written.

CHAPTER 4

How to pray
Finding a friend

First impressions matter. At least, that is apparently true in speed dating! But relationships that are really important to us necessarily go beyond first impressions – modifying them or confirming them. It takes time to develop a mature relationship. Friends, they say, don't grow on trees. Neither are lasting friendships made in an instant.

There are some people whose first real experience of God is so instant, so dramatic, so overwhelming that it knocks them out – it is life-changing. That's what seems to have happened to St Paul while he was on a journey to Damascus and he was confronted by a vision of Jesus. But for many people, getting to know God is a gradual, even a lifetime, experience. The relationship with God builds up – through reading the Bible, by talking about him to other people, through worship, through prayer.

As we saw in chapter 3 – 'What is prayer?' – having a developing relationship with God is really the main purpose of prayer. But if that is the 'What', help may still be needed when it comes to the 'How'.

Is anybody there?

It ought to be child's play, something very natural. And in some ways it is – just talking and listening to God, like you would to a friend. Except your friend is not invisible. Even if they are a long way away you can talk on the phone and hear their voice.

It's not quite the same with God – or at least not all the time, or very often. It can sometimes feel as though we are talking to the air or just listening to our own thoughts. There is a joke about an old Jewish man who had been going to the Western Wall in Jerusalem (a sacred place of prayer and pilgrimage for Jews) every day for 60 years to pray for peace between Christians, Jews and Muslims and that the hatred between them would cease. When asked how it felt, he replied, 'Like praying to a wall.' Fortunately, what we feel is not the whole story.

Arrow prayers

It can be a sign of a good relationship that we are able to get in touch with a friend for a really quick conversation – perhaps a simple request such as 'How about lunch on Monday?', 'Can I borrow your lawnmower?' or 'Are you going to the match?' Text messaging encourages such brevity. But it's hardly the best way to develop a friendship.

Quick, brief prayers shot out like **arrows** in the midst of a busy life can feel very helpful and reflect a sense that there is no time that is too busy for God, no matter too trivial, no situation in which he cannot be included. They may be a request for someone else or for ourselves. They may be a sudden burst of gratitude or amazement at the goodness of God. Short as they are, they are not to be despised, although it would be odd if this were the only way we prayed.

Finding time

Developing a friendship takes time – so does praying. So give yourself time – regularly. The founder of Methodism, John Wesley, used to say that when he was really busy he would pray for four hours a day. Few Christians are able to follow that example or would even attempt it. We are more likely to be tempted to say that we are very busy and can only spare a few minutes. That may say something about our priorities, but if that's being realistic then at least start there and stick to it. You may be amazed how you find yourself just wanting to spend more time in prayer.

Where to pray

Jesus suggested to his friends that when they prayed they should find somewhere private and quiet. This allows us to give more attention to what we are doing when we pray. For the same reason, some people find it helpful to fold their hands (it stops them fidgeting) and to close their eyes or to focus on a particular picture or object, like a lighted candle. We can be distracted all too easily, so these are simple aids to help us focus on what we are doing and who we are praying to.

Are you sitting comfortably?

We should also try to help the body be still and quiet. That means finding a position that helps you to relax but remain attentive. It will not help if you are tense or uncomfortable, but neither does it help to slouch! Most people like to sit in an upright chair in which they feel supported but not rigid. Others prefer the more traditional posture of kneeling, or standing or even lying prostrate. Find what suits you best.

There are various ways that we can become relaxed. One way is to breathe slowly and deeply while consciously relaxing the muscles, starting at the top of the head and gradually working down to the soles of the feet. With a bit of practice you should find this quite easy to do.

It's perhaps less easy to relax the mind. The more we try to empty our heads of all intrusive thoughts, the more they tend to rush in. It is sometimes suggested that the best way is not to try and get rid of such thoughts but just to ignore them. Perhaps an easier way is to give relaxed attention to one thing that will lead into prayer. This is where an object like a candle or a picture of a crucifix can be helpful. Others find helpful the repetition of a mantra like the Jesus prayer: 'Lord Jesus Christ, Son of God, have mercy on me,' or 'In God I trust and will not fear.'

A.C.T.S.

We don't spend all our time asking things of our friends, so although asking God for things is understandable and OK, it shouldn't be the only part of praying. As a simple reminder that prayer is more than just asking, we might use the Acronym ACTS – Adoration, Confession, Thanksgiving, Supplication. (See chapter 3 – 'What is prayer?')

Supplication is a fancy way of saying 'asking' – asking for things, for others as well as for ourselves. When Jesus told his friends to ask God the Father for anything, he added that it should be in his name (John 16:23). He didn't mean that we should simply tag his name on to the bottom of a request, although many written prayers do end, 'in the name of Jesus Christ our Lord.' More significantly, it means that we should consider asking for those things that Jesus would want for us or for others. It is part of how we can develop, as we see our prayers, and indeed our whole lives, from God's point of view – that is, a point of view that wants the very best for us and wants what will help us to become the most fully human we can be. And in the Christian faith, the model for what it means to be fully human is Jesus.

If we have heard formal prayers in a church service or read them in a prayer book, we might think that we have to use a special sort of language to make prayers 'proper'. It isn't so. Just be natural. If it doesn't come out quite right, just have another go. We don't always find it easy to speak of important things to our friends – we may stumble a bit and have to phrase it in a different way. It's no different when we talk with God.

Some people find it helpful to use a book of prayers. Certain people have the knack of writing prayers that say just what we want to say but couldn't have put into words ourself. Sometimes the prayers of others act as a reminder of what we should be praying for. Organisations such as Christian Aid offer books of prayers that highlight concerns and needs in places we might not be aware of. Prayers for others are not only for their benefit – they also help to enlarge our own loving concern.

Praying with the Bible

Since one of the purposes of prayer is to get to know God better, it can be helpful to make use of the Bible, which tells us quite a lot about God. It is possible to buy small books or find resources online that offer lists of biblical passages that have been found to be particularly helpful in this way. Or you may like to take just a few verses from a psalm – for example, Psalm 23.

- First ask God to guide you in your reading and thinking by his Holy Spirit (see chapter 9 – 'Holy Spirit') so that you may be open to what he is saying to you through the words of Scripture.

- Read the passage to get a general feel of what it is saying.

- Then read it again more slowly and choose a very short section which will become the focus for your thoughts and reflection.

- Use your imagination and don't be afraid to be playful in your meditation.

- Turn your thoughts into prayer – of thanks, adoration, confession or supplication – or into silent awareness of God's presence.

There are many different guides and systems on how to pray. What has been offered here is just a taster. In the end, the method is less important than the doing and the growing in that relationship which is the focus of prayer – a loving relationship with the loving God.

CHAPTER 5

Going to church

A strange experience

Most church congregations will say that they are very welcoming to strangers. That's not always how the strangers find it.

What to do

Whether the church is welcoming or not, attending a church service for the first time can feel quite daunting. It's probably best if you go with someone – but that is not always possible. You may not know anyone who goes to the church.

You are not quite sure what you are supposed to do and you don't want either to embarrass yourself or to upset others. Will you know when to stand and when to sit down? Do you have to kneel? Which book are you supposed to use and how will you find the right place? It feels as bad as going to a very posh banquet and not knowing which cutlery to use. Will everyone glare at you if you get it wrong?

At their best, churches will normally have someone who is on the lookout for newcomers. They will know that you might be feeling a bit nervous and will try to be helpful without being 'pushy'. Being smothered can feel just as bad as being ignored. They should help you to find somewhere to sit and tell you what books or papers you will need for the service. They might ask if you would like them to sit with you and then sensitively guide you through the service.

Old-fashioned

If you have never actually been inside a church before, the building itself may feel strange, especially if it is 'old-fashioned'. Much of the action may be happening quite a long way away from where you are sitting – and most newcomers feel more at ease sitting at the back than at the front. There may be bits of furniture you don't quite recognise, and if the church has pews rather than seats you may not be feeling particularly comfortable.

Worship

Unless you have gone into a church to be quietly on your own or are there for a concert, the chances are that you have gone to an act of worship – a service of some kind. It may be a baptism, a wedding or a funeral, in which case you will have some notion of what it's for. But an 'ordinary' act of worship – a service – is not so obvious.

What is 'worship'? The origin of the word is 'worth-ship' – giving worth, in this case to God. Worshippers are seeking to express their sense of God's worth, his value in their lives, to give God praise and thanks, to say sorry for their wrongdoing, to listen to what God is wanting to say to them through the Bible or a sermon, and they are inviting him to come to them in the power of his Holy Spirit (see chapter 9 – 'Holy Spirit'). Sometimes the service will be very formal, set out in a book which the worshippers follow. At other times it will be much more spontaneous, following the direction of the worship leader (see chapter 15 – 'Worship and church services').

When the worship begins it is likely that there will be quite a lot that is unfamiliar. Traditional worship might feel a bit austere, while some 'modern' worship can feel a bit over-exuberant. Some people prefer organs and choirs; others like guitars and singing groups. For some it is the sense of awe and quiet that suits them, while others like worship to be lively and loud. There is no one correct way to worship. It depends on taste – and flavours vary. Some foods take a bit of getting used to but then become a favourite. The same is true of worship, so it's worth sticking with it, giving it a good try before deciding whether one form or another is not for you.

Unless you already know some hymns or worship songs, one of the main ways of people participating together – singing – will only make you feel more out of it. But you will find it quite amazing how quickly you will pick tunes up, and in some churches songs or choruses are repeated several times, which can help.

Why go to church?

It is worth reminding yourself why you have gone to church. No one has forced you. You are there because you have chosen to go. The reasons may be very varied, and each could affect the way you are feeling at the time. It may be that some friends have suggested you go along with them and they have already told you a bit about what will go on. Or you may have popped in on the spur of the moment because you felt that it could be helpful because you are facing a difficult time. You may have lost someone close and it feels like a way of paying respects, or of finding comfort. You may fancy the vicar! In all this, you may most significantly be looking for a way to find God.

The first time you go to a church might be for a special occasion, not so much for yourself as in support of friends – perhaps for a christening, a wedding or a funeral. It may feel little more than a social occasion. Your expectations, if you have any, may focus more upon who you are there for rather than anything specifically 'spiritual'. But hopefully it will be a good occasion – a way of celebrating or of sharing and expressing grief. You may glimpse something you had not expected.

Powerful

Worship has the power to move us and to raise our spirits. You may be feeling lonely, but in worship you are not alone: others are present. Their faith may give you strength in your search. The concerns that are expressed through prayer and fellowship can be a comfort – not because they are specifically about you but because there is a tangible atmosphere of loving care. Some of the language used may be strange to you – some of it may even sound fanciful – but it can help to put you in touch with something that is beyond you.

The reading from the Bible may sound like something from a bygone age yet resonate with where you are and what your spirit needs. The sermon or address may at times go above your head yet speak to your heart.

Going to a church service for the first time may well feel strange – but it can also be exciting, eye-opening and heart-warming. There may be no more than a stirring, a hesitant feeling that this is right – it feels good. Hopefully something will happen, a word will be said that encourages you to go again and perhaps even to become part of a worshipping community. Why not give it a go?

CHAPTER 6

Church buildings

More than heritage

Churches are part of the landscape – both rural and urban. Traditional-style churches are everywhere. In villages the church will most often be medieval – in towns they are more likely to be Victorian or later. Modern churches, because they don't follow the usual pattern of having a tower or spire, may be less easy to recognise.

Both Catholics and Anglicans have 'parish' churches – they serve a geographical area known as a parish. All churches that were built before the Reformation (before the sixteenth century) belonged to the Roman Catholic Church, but after Henry VIII broke the English Church away from Rome they were taken over by the Church of England. During the centuries since that time, churches and chapels have been constructed by various denominations such as Baptists, Methodists, Presbyterians and Congregationalists. The Salvation Army has what they call Citadels, and Quakers use Meeting Houses. Catholics also built churches again as they regained the freedom to worship openly.

The size and design of church buildings vary considerably – from simple thatched country churches with round towers and room for less than 100 worshippers to buildings that will hold 1000 and that have a plethora of spires, turrets, buttresses and columns. There is no one set design, although the overall plan of traditional churches is basically similar. They are usually oblong or square (although there is a famous round church in Cambridge) with a general sitting area filled with seats or pews. This is known as the **nave** and it faces to the east where there will be a place where the choir traditionally sits. This is known as the **chancel** or

choir, and beyond it is the focus of the whole building where the altar or Holy Table stands in the **sanctuary**. Where there are side aisles and crossing ways, the floor plan of a church may look like a cross – recalling the cross on which Jesus died.

Newly formed or very small congregations do not always have the resources to provide their own buildings, at least not initially. They have therefore made use of whatever suitable building has been available. Some congregations will share a church building of another denomination, use a school or community hall or rent buildings that have otherwise become disused, e.g. a cinema. Many of the black-led churches have started in such a way but some have grown considerably over the years, developing their own resources and able to acquire their own building complexes. As the name implies 'house churches' are gatherings (usually quite small) of Christians in someone's home, the way early Christians met (1 Corinthians 16:19). Many house churches developed in the 1970s largely through members breaking away from congregations of mainstream churches to worship more freely and be independent from other church structures. The numbers of these churches expanded considerably over the years and became what are now sometimes called 'New Churches.'

Spaces

Churches, like all buildings, are fundamentally just enclosed spaces. It is what goes on in that space that dictates how the building is arranged. The design referred to above reflects the fact that people like to have seats when they attend worship. This was not always so, and in some traditions it still isn't. While the priests conducted the worship, people stood around or moved about. Some seating was provided around the walls for those who were too infirm to remain standing, and one theory for the origin of the saying 'the weak go to the wall' comes from this practice.

As well as seats, there are in most churches other pieces of furniture for specific purposes. These will normally reflect the worshipping life of the church, although increasingly even in ancient parish churches provision is also made for some community use, e.g. by the provision of kitchen facilities. An altar or holy table (see below) will have a prominent place in those churches where the service of Holy Communion is central to the worship. Pulpits (see below) will have pride of place where preaching is given high priority. And in those churches where the worship is more informal it may well be that the raised dais for the choir and music group will be most obvious. Traditionally, one of the simplest spaces for church members to gather in has been the plain setting of the Friends' (Quakers) meeting. Where congregations meet in a borrowed hall there may be little specific provision for them unless it is portable!

The altar

The main worship of many churches is the service variously known as the Lord's Supper, Holy Communion, the Mass or the Eucharist. The service recalls the final occasion when Jesus had supper with his friends, on the night before he was arrested, tried and executed. The altar or table is the focus of this service when the church members share symbolically in the meal by receiving a small piece of bread (or a wafer) and a sip of wine. They recall the sacrifice that was made by Jesus on behalf of everyone – an outpouring of selfless love for the forgiveness of wrongdoing (sin).

The table or altar is normally at the east end of the church. This reminds worshippers that they are facing the direction of the rising sun, recalling the resurrection of Jesus from the dead.

The pulpit

In some churches where the emphasis is less on the service of Holy Communion and more on preaching and teaching from the Bible and through sermons, the pulpit will be most prominent. This is usually a raised, quite small, enclosed 'box' in which the preacher stands to deliver the sermon or to read from the Bible.

The font

Traditionally, just inside the entrance of the church would be the 'font' where baptisms take place. 'Font' comes from a Latin word meaning 'spring of water' and reflects the fact that water is used for baptisms, which derive from a form of religious washing. Baptism recalls the baptism of Christ and is a ritual by which a person becomes a member of the church.

The font was placed at the entrance of the church as a sign that it is through baptism that one 'enters' the church. In larger churches it has its own area, known as the baptistery. In modern times, many fonts are placed at the front of the nave so that people can see what is going on. Small portable fonts are also sometimes used.

In Baptist churches where baptism takes place by being fully immersed in water, the font is replaced with a baptising pool or tank set into the floor of the church.

Some churches have felt that having the priest or minister a long way away at the far end of the church where the altar/table is placed makes them too remote, so they designed their buildings to create worship 'in the round'. In this arrangement the seats are placed either literally in a circle around the altar/table or in large semicircles. Everyone can see what is happening more easily and worshippers can feel that they are not simply passive observers but are more actively taking part in the worship. A famous church with this arrangement is the modern Roman Catholic Cathedral in

Liverpool, known affectionately as 'Paddy's wigwam' because of its external appearance.

Cathedral

A cathedral is the main or 'mother' church of a diocese – an area in the Catholic or Anglican Church similar in size to a county or two. It is usually a large and imposing building. Some, such as Durham Cathedral, are world heritage sites.

The name 'cathedral' comes from the Latin for a seat or throne (*cathedra*) and it is the building where the leader of a diocese – the bishop – has his seat. In the past it would also have been where the bishop held court to make judgements on wrongdoers who were brought before him.

Community use

Millions of people visit churches and cathedrals to admire the architecture, the stained-glass windows, the wonderful gothic roofs or the mighty columns in the nave. Churches are a major part of our national built heritage and in England 14,500 worship buildings are listed as of architectural and historical value. Around 85 per cent of these are Anglican churches. They are beautiful and culturally significant. But, more importantly, they are places of living worship, standing as witnesses to the presence of God in a place.

In many rural areas the church is the only public building in the community, and in more recent years many have recovered something of their use for the community as well as being a worship space. They are places to meet one another as well as to meet God, places in which to serve neighbour as well as to serve God. They are used for concerts, for drama productions, for old people's lunches, for mums and toddler groups, for meetings and even, occasionally, for post offices. This is felt to be very modern – in fact, it reflects what happened in medieval times.

CHAPTER 7

God

Father, Creator

As far as we can tell, human beings have always believed in gods – gods of thunder and lightning, gods of war and peace, gods of fertility and harvest. Archaeological evidence indicates that religious rituals were present in pre-historical times, related not only to crops and to hunting but also, and most obviously, to life and death. Christians, along with religions like Judaism and Islam, believe that there is only one God.

All our efforts to understand, to explain and to describe God in the end fail. We cannot fully pin him down. God is mystery. The best we can do is use words and images, pictures and music, our feelings and our minds to try to express what God is like. No single one of them is enough. Even saying that God is Father is using an image: it is the image produced by a patriarchal society and has its limitations. It is not just feminists who insist that the image of God as Mother is also true to what God is like. The prophet Isaiah described God as Mother (Isaiah 66:13), and the medieval nun Dame Julian of Norwich called Jesus 'our Mother'. Such descriptions remind us of both the richness and the limitations of imagery.

Speaking about God

Just because we cannot say everything about God doesn't mean we can say nothing or that it is all simply made up. Christians believe that God helps us to know what he is like. He shows us through the world of nature, through events in history, through the Bible and through personal experience. This 'showing' is called 'revelation' – God reveals himself; we don't only have to rely on our own efforts. It is this that places limits upon what we do say about God. We cannot just believe anything we like – it has to 'fit' with the Bible, the Church's teaching and our own spiritual experience, which are where God 'reveals' himself.

But most distinctively, it is through the person of Jesus that we get to know what God is most fully like. **Jesus** is understood to be the way God has expressed himself – in human form. This is why Jesus is sometimes referred to as the Word – see John 1:1. He wasn't just a good man but was himself, within the constraints of being human, what God is. That is why he is called the Son of God (see chapter 8 – 'Jesus'). This title is also using imagery – Christians don't believe that Jesus is God's son in a biological, sexual way. It is the closeness of their relationship and of the way they are and behave that is being expressed.

Christians believe that God is **Creator**. It was God, not chance, that brought our universe, and all other universes, into existence. Things are the way they are because that is the way God created them, and that includes the laws of nature that science explores and explains. The book of Genesis in the Bible is just one attempt to convey in terms of a story what happened. Science presents a quite different account of the process, and the majority of Christians are happy to find truth in both – spiritual truth in the Genesis story and scientific truth in the insights of cosmology.

God continues to care about his creation – including human beings. We can have a special relationship with God. This means that the more we know about God, the more we can know about ourselves. The Bible says that we are made in his image; he is not made in ours. Most importantly, this means that we can relate to God as he relates to us. The relationship is one of care and nurture, of love and challenge. Jesus had that relationship in a unique way but he says that we can share it, and that the most appropriate way of describing God is as Abba – which means '**Dad**'.

The simplest but most profound description of God is that '**God is love**' (1 John 4:16). We discover what true love is like the more we understand what God's love is like. For Christians, God's love is outgoing, inclusive of all, and self-giving. It was that outgoing love that made God want to create. It is his all-inclusive love that gives everyone value and worth, no matter what or who they are. It is his self-giving love that we see expressed in Jesus' selfless life and his willingness to die for others.

Restoring relationships

God loves us and wants us to freely love him in a way that expresses that love and makes our lives as fully human as possible. Experience shows us that human beings find it quite hard to live up to this expectation. We get things wrong – in our relationships with one another as well as in our relationship with God.

Relationships go wrong in big and small ways. We fail to be loving all the time. In religious terms that failure is known as **sin**. In small and in big ways it means that there is a break in relationships and we are not doing or being what God wants us to do and be. In his love, God wants to mend those relationships – with him and between men and women. It takes forgiveness, and forgiveness is costly. God is willing to take that cost upon himself – and that is what we see in Jesus' dying on the cross. Love ultimately wins through, and this is what Jesus' resurrection tells us. It is why he is described as Saviour and Rescuer – because he rescues us from the consequences of sin (see chapter 14 – 'Sin and forgiveness').

God not only forgives, he also helps us in our efforts to live loving lives. Christians believe that he guides us and enables us in the depths of our being, spiritually. This is God the loving sustainer at work.

CHAPTER 8

Jesus

Saviour, Friend

Christians follow **Jesus of Nazareth** – a Jewish religious leader who lived about 2000 years ago in what we now call Israel, when the country was under the control of the Romans. The town of Nazareth is situated in the northern part of the country around Lake Galilee.

Jesus' followers believed that he was God's special agent who would bring in a time when God's rule would be seen and known on Earth. Jews had long believed that this would happen and that the person would be appointed or 'anointed' by God for this task. In Hebrew the title for the 'anointed one' was 'Messiah', and in Greek it was 'Christos', and it is from this that Christians take their name. 'Christ' is a title, not a surname – it speaks of Jesus' role or job – rather like how in Wales people speak of 'Jones the Butcher' or 'Williams the Bread'. So Jesus was **Jesus the Christ** – Jesus the anointed one.

Starting out

For 30 years Jesus lived with his parents, Mary and Joseph, in Nazareth, and later perhaps in the town of Capernaum on Lake Galilee. His father was a tradesman – a carpenter – and Jesus learnt this trade. Virtually nothing is known about what Jesus did during those 30 years. He is not thought to have married.

He first appeared on the public scene at the River Jordan where his cousin John (John the Baptist) was conducting mass washings or 'baptisms' as a sign of repentance and religious renewal. Jesus' **baptism** was a significant moment for him – it confirmed his belief that God was calling him to a life of teaching, preaching and healing to announce the coming of God's rule – his kingdom. It was the start of about three years as a travelling preacher.

Disciples

Like other religious leaders, Jesus collected a number of followers. The closest group who stayed with him were called 'disciples' and traditionally there were 12 of them (making reference to the 12 tribes of Israel). The disciples included Peter, whose name meant 'rocky'; John, who seems to have been a particular favourite; John's brother James; and Judas, who was later to 'betray' Jesus to the authorities.

To start with, Jesus seems to have concentrated his efforts in the area of Galilee where he built up a considerable reputation both as a teacher and as a healer and exorcist. He was particularly good at telling stories about everyday things, such as shepherds and sheep, sowing and reaping, building a house, being robbed and beaten up, weddings, and jealousy among brothers. But he used the stories he told (which he called 'parables') to make people think about what God was like and what life would be like in **God's kingdom**.

Jesus would have read the Jewish Scriptures (what Christians call the Old Testament of the Bible); he would have prayed daily and attended worship in the local **synagogue** on the Sabbath (Saturday).

Prayer

Jesus was a devout Jew but he had his own ideas, and while his teaching drew quite a following among the people, he was increasingly at odds with the religious authorities. He had a very close relationship with God, whom he called Daddy (*Abba* –

'Father'). He taught his disciples to pray to God with a prayer that begins, '**Our Father** in heaven . . .' (Matthew 6:9).

God was at work in Jesus in such a uniquely powerful way that his followers came to believe that he was in fact God in human form (incarnate). They called him the '**Son of God**' and '**Lord**' and later worshipped him as equal to God.

It is unlikely that Jesus made such claims for himself. He seems to have seen himself as a prophet proclaiming the word of God, and he described himself either as the Son of Man (a representative of humanity) or **the Servant** – a figure described in the Old Testament (in the book of the prophet Isaiah) who served God and the people but was rejected and suffered for the people.

Trouble brewing

The religious authorities were worried by Jesus' popularity and his talk of God's kingdom. They thought the Romans would see it as insurrection, and they didn't want to annoy the Romans. On a visit to Jerusalem Jesus went to **the Temple** (the centre of Jewish religion) and caused a stir by upsetting the tables of the traders who were selling animals for sacrifice. He seemed to be threatening all that the Temple stood for.

With the help of information from the disciple Judas, the authorities had Jesus arrested at night, held an investigation and sent him to the Roman ruler (Pontius Pilate), demanding the death penalty. Pilate had Jesus scourged and eventually sentenced him to death by crucifixion. This is remembered on **Good Friday**.

Three days later, and on a number of other occasions over a 40-day period, Jesus appeared to his disciples – not as a ghost but alive again in a new way. This was 'resurrection' (**Easter Day**).

This is the unique and vital Christian belief – that Jesus truly died but was alive again. It was not resuscitation. He then left them to be with God in heaven (the **Ascension**). What had been a disaster on Good Friday came to be seen as a victory over death. His crucifixion was not simply seen as the execution of a criminal but was also understood to be instrumental in bringing God's forgiveness for all people. His followers believed that God had been behind all this and that he then gave them his Holy Spirit to help them spread the message about Jesus (**Pentecost**). This was the beginning of the Christian Church.

The story of Jesus appears in the second part of the Bible called the **New Testament**, and in particular in the four accounts called **Gospels**. There is very little reference to Jesus in other contemporary writing. Only two of the Gospels (Matthew and Luke) tell the story of his birth. It was believed that his mother, Mary, was a virgin and became pregnant through the power of God (the Holy Spirit). The events remembered at Christmas are a combination of the stories in the early chapters of these two Gospels.

Jesus' CV

(The references are from one of the Gospels, the one written by Luke, and from the Acts of the Apostles which was also written by Luke.)

Title	Lord, Christ, Messiah
Marital status	Single
Nationality	Jew
Born	In Bethlehem around 4 BC *Luke 1, 2*
Parents	Joseph and Mary

Brought up   In Nazareth in Galilee
Luke 2:39, 40

Early years   Visits Jerusalem as a 12-year-old
Luke 2:41-52

Job   Carpenter and later itinerant preacher and healer

Baptised   Baptised in the River Jordan at the age of 30 by John the Baptist
Luke 3:1-23

Job induction   Six weeks fasting in the desert
Luke 4:1-13

Friends   Twelve close friends and also friendly with prostitutes and people on the edge of society

Career   Three years travelling around the country preaching, teaching and healing
Luke 4:14–19:28

High point   Enters Jerusalem riding on a donkey
Luke 19:29-47

Social life   Has a final evening meal with his friends
Luke 22:1-38

Criminal record   Arrested in an olive grove known as the Garden of Gethsemane
Luke 22:39-54

Court appearances	Appeared before the Jewish religious authorities *Luke 22:66-71* Trial in front of the Roman ruler Pontius Pilate *Luke 23:1-25*
Executed	Crucified on Skull Hill (Golgotha) *Luke 23:26-49*
Other relevant information	Was alive again and seen by his friends *Luke 24:1-49* Appeared to various followers in different places for a period of about six weeks
Last seen	On Mount Olivet *Acts1:1-14*

CHAPTER 9

Holy Spirit

God in action

Jesus once told a woman he met on a journey that 'God is spirit' (John 4:24). It is important to note that he did not say 'God is *a* spirit,' as though God is one spirit among many. Spirit is what God is, the way God is, or, to put it more crudely, it's what God is made of. The very difficulty we have in trying to explain this points to the fact that what is 'spiritual' is mysterious, different from experience in the everyday, physical world around us. It's not made any easier because ideas about 'spirits' have the notion of things that are spooky.

In the Christian understanding of the person of God (see section on 'Trinity' later in this chapter), we used to talk about God as Father, Son and Holy **Ghost**. And that, of course, made it sound as if this third person of the Trinity was also something rather spooky. These days we speak of the Holy **Spirit** – Holy to show that we are talking about God, and Spirit to show that we are talking about something that is other than physical. In religious art the Holy Spirit is often depicted as a dove (see Luke 3:21, 22).

Creation

The Christian understanding of God as 'spirit' has its roots in the Jewish belief that the God they worshipped was not like the gods of the countries around them that were displayed in the form of idols of wood or stone. Rather, their God was above and beyond this world of time and space although also very involved in it. They viewed this aspect of God at work in his world and throughout his creation as the activity of the 'Spirit' of God. So in the account of creation that we have in the book of Genesis (the first book of the Bible) it is the Spirit of God who moves across the watery chaos to bring order and shape to creation (Genesis 1:1, 2). The word for Spirit was the same word as 'wind' or 'breath', and so the 'spirit' of God, the 'breath' of God, is understood to be what gives life. We are told that God 'breathed' into the man he formed out of the dust, and that it was the 'breath of life' (Genesis 2:7).

God's activity was also seen in the way he communicated with people. Sometimes he is said to have visited them through messengers (angels), but often he spoke to them more directly by his Spirit – he '**inspired**', 'in-spirited', them. It was by his Spirit that God **blessed** people, and if he took his spirit away from them (as he did from King Saul), their well-being and good fortune declined. So the Spirit was also associated with God's action in **judgement**.

The Spirit was also involved in **guiding** people to act in the way God wanted. Wherever God was seen to be active it was believed that the Spirit of God was present. A simple but not inaccurate way of describing the Spirit is to say the Spirit is 'God in action'.

The work of the Holy Spirit is seen even more clearly in the writings of the **New Testament**. Mary was told by the angel that the Holy Spirit would come upon her and as a result she would have a child – Jesus (Luke 1:35). When Jesus was baptised by John we are told that the Holy Spirit descended upon him in the form of a dove (Luke 3:21, 22). It was the Holy Spirit that led Jesus into the wilderness where he spent 40 days fasting and praying and where he suffered three great temptations (Luke 4:1-13).

Pentecost

On the night before he died, Jesus promised his disciples that although he was leaving them he would send the Holy Spirit ('the Spirit of truth') to be with them (John 15:26). This was fulfilled at the event the Church remembers at Pentecost or 'Whit Sunday'. The account of this outpouring of the Holy Spirit upon the disciples appears in chapter 2 of the book of Acts. St Luke, who wrote the book of Acts, went on to describe the spread of the Church as St Paul and others journeyed across the eastern Mediterranean, and he reports that this missionary work was guided and empowered by the Holy Spirit.

Christians understand that God's Spirit 'lives' within them, helping them to the live in the way Jesus would want them to. The Spirit guides them and helps them in their prayers – even when they don't know what to ask for. The work of the Spirit in someone's life is not just a private matter but shows itself in the way that person behaves and the characteristics they display. St Paul described these as the **fruit of the spirit**, and they include love, joy, peace, patience, kindness, generosity, faithfulness, gentleness and self-control (Galatians 5:22, 23).

Along with the fruit of the Spirit are the **gifts of the Spirit**. Traditionally, these have been understood to be wisdom, understanding, wonder and awe, right judgement, knowledge, courage and reverence. They are based on a passage from the Old Testament (Isaiah 11:2, 3). In the New Testament other gifts are identified, and there are various lists of them in Paul's writings – see Romans 12:6-8, 1 Corinthians 12:8-10 and Ephesians 4:11. Some of these gifts are to do with the individual's life, such as faith and mercy; others are related to work within the Church (such as teaching and prophecy) or with helping people in need (healing). The purpose of such gifts is to build up the Church and its people so that they can serve the purposes of God all the better. It is unfortunate that at times the possession of such gifts has been seen either as the only proof of true faith or as a way for people to gain power within the life of the Church. The gifts of the Spirit are for service of others, not for personal status.

The Trinity

God the Father/Creator, God the Son/Saviour, God the Sustainer/ Spirit – not three gods but one God understood and experienced in these different ways – as different aspects of Love. It is mystery in the end. And the only way to express it is through imagery. God is three but is one – that is what God as Trinity describes. It is not meant to be a mathematical puzzle but is the best way we can manage to express that divine relationship of love that Father, Son and Holy Spirit are.

To help us understand it we might think of how one person can have different roles – for example, a woman might be a daughter, a mother and a wife. St Augustine described it in this way: God is love: the Father is the lover, the Son is the Beloved, and the Holy Spirit is the love they have for each other.[2] When it comes to God – relationship is everything.

---

2. St Augustine, *De Trinitate* Book 8

CHAPTER 10

Love

It's all that matters

'All you need,' sang the Beatles, 'is love.' And Christians would agree. No matter what the show *Cabaret* declared, it's love, not money, that makes the world go around.

There's a lot of it about. Or, at least, there's a lot of talk about love. We hear the word all over the place – people love their pop idols, their hairdo, the latest car, the family dog, a favourite restaurant. As often as not it means, 'I like it a lot'. But love has a much deeper and richer meaning than that.

For the Christian, it starts from what John wrote in a letter to some early Christians: 'God is love.' Love comes from God, and that is why we should love one another. According to John, the degree to which we love other people is the measure for how much we know and love God (1 John 4:7, 8). It is love, not power, that is the key characteristic of the God in whom Christians believe. It is important to be as clear as possible just what kind of love this is.

Love for all

According to the prophet Jeremiah, God told his people that he loved them with an everlasting love (Jeremiah 31:3). The people experienced this love as God's commitment to them. God stuck by his people in the good times and the bad times, when they were faithful and when they were disobedient. His love was expressed in his mercy and his judgement, in his rescuing them and in his punishing them. It is important to understand that judgement and punishment are grounded in love, not revenge or anger. God's judgement is a loving judgement – it seeks not the destruction of others but their transformation. His punishment is a loving punishment – seeking to correct and lead his people to renewed and reformed lives, not to destroyed lives. That understanding was something that only gradually dawned on people. They often saw God as wrathful rather than loving, as angry rather than merciful. But through insights given by the prophets and, most powerfully, in the life, death and resurrection of Jesus, the deeply serious and multifaceted nature of God's love became better understood.

In Jesus, this love was seen to go deeper than even the prophets had perceived. St John tells us that it was out of love not just for the Jewish people but for the whole world that he sent his Son on a rescue mission (John 3:16). Jesus' death on the cross 'for the sins of the world'[3] was an expression of God's self-giving, sacrificial love. He was, as it were, willing to give himself away for the sake of others.

Love for others

So God's love is creative; it is seen in commitment and in self-giving. It is this kind of love that Christians are called to show in their lives. Such love is not simply a matter of nice feelings. Feelings are important but can get you only so far. Love like this also involves an active choice of will. It gives value and worth to the other, it motivates good action even when it is costly, it puts the needs of others before one's own desires. It is this kind of love that Jesus was thinking of when he told his disciples that all the rules, all the commandments, are summed up in two simple guidelines: Love God; Love your neighbour (other people). Such love is the basis, the motivation, the driving force of being fully human and creating a fully human community.

---

3. Commonly used phrase. Also see John 1:29.

The love Jesus showed was the love of the father going out to welcome a son who had wasted all the family inheritance, led a bad life and been an embarrassment all round (the story of the prodigal son, Luke 15:11-32). It is the love of the shepherd who goes after a lost sheep (Luke 15:3-7). It is the love that forgives those who hurt you (Luke 23:34) and goes out of one's way to care for those in need (Luke 8:40-56). It is the love of the preacher who held out a hand to lepers (Matthew 8:2-4) and who risked his reputation by meeting with people who were shunned by the respectable (Matthew 9:10-13). It is the love Jesus showed to God his Father by being willing to do what love demanded, even though it would cost him his life (Matthew 26:36-46).

For Christians, Jesus is the supreme example of what it means to be a fully loving person.

CHAPTER 11

Good and evil

A mixed-up world

Christians believe that this is a good world – it's God's world. There is an order to the world as science shows us through the laws of nature, and order is good. Continuous chaos would make life as we know it impossible and would certainly not be good. There is a beauty in the world – we delight in splendid views, in glorious sunsets, in the song of birds and the variety of animal life. In the Genesis story, when God looked at what he had created, he saw it was good. There is so much that is good in our lives as individuals and as part of society. Good relationships are deeply rewarding and make us feel good. God wants life to be good and fulfilling for everyone – and for many it is.

But not for all – not everywhere, not always. However much we delight in what is good we also know that there are some terrible things in the world – there is pain and violence, there is ugliness and destruction, there is crime and disease, and nature can be very cruel. In any realistic view of our world and our lives we have to account for both what is wonderful and what is awful, what is good and what is evil.

The way things are

We could just give a resigned shrug of our shoulders and say, 'That's the way things are – you just have to get on with it.' That's easier if life is treating us kindly, less easy if we are at the bottom of the heap.

Something can be good because it pleases our senses (aesthetically good), because it does what it is meant to do (functionally good), because it behaves in a way that is creative and helpful (morally good), because it enhances the human spirit and is pleasing to God (spiritually good). When Christians say the world is good, it can include all of these things.

Something can be wrong (or evil) when it is ugly, it doesn't work as it should, when it offends the moral norm or when it disobeys the intention God had for it. And the world can be wrong in all these ways.

From our viewpoint

When we say things are good or bad, we are most often viewing them from our human perspective – are they good or bad for us? It doesn't mean they are essentially bad or good in themselves. A mountain, for example, can be very beautiful and we might say it is good. But if it suddenly erupts and spews molten lava on a town below, killing lots of people, we would say this is a wrong. If people are not involved, the mountain and its eruption are neutral. In fact, eruptions actually do good to the world in the sense that they are part of the renewal of its mineral resources. We talk of good weather and bad weather, depending on how we experience it. But the weather is just part of the meteorological working of the atmosphere.

In the Bible there are many stories that involve the impact of nature upon the lives of men and women, and indeed of nations. Earthquakes and storms, eruptions and epidemics were seen as God's activity, usually as punishment for the disobedience of the people. Some people still see things that way, although usually we accept the more scientific explanation. However, as the green movement and those concerned about global warming tell us, there is a connection between the way we behave, how we exploit the planet, and some of the activity in nature. The wrong is not so much nature's fault as ours. God, it might be said, has set up our world in such a way that human beings need to respect it and steward it, not selfishly exploit it. The consequences are built in.

Our fault

The story of the Fall in Genesis puts the blame for things going wrong squarely on the shoulders of human beings. Their act of disobedience upset the good order of things. The stories that follow show how that disorder resulted in jealousy, murder, pride and the division of families and nations. The wrong, as well as the good in our world, is down to us! And we find it hard to maintain good order and peace (harmony). The evidence is in front of us on the television and in the newspapers every day. Nowhere and no one is exempt. Wrongdoing is global!

Bias to the wrong

Drawing upon the insight of that story in Genesis, Christians see this as basically a spiritual matter – our failure to be the kind of people God wants us to be and to do the things he wants us to do. We choose to be what we want to be and to do things our way, and that isn't always for the good. There seems to be a bias in us that drags us towards wrongdoing. Scientists might well say that this is in fact our evolutionary background – we carry with us traits of aggression and defence of our territory which made survival possible at earlier stages. Christians may agree there is some truth in that, but would still want to add that it is also a spiritual matter that is true for all human beings. Wrongdoing is in our spiritual nature as well as in our genes!

The devil

But is all the responsibility ours? Often our conscience tells us we are making a wrong choice, but sometimes we seem to do things that we don't really want to. There is the tradition that this is where the 'devil' comes in. The devil is thought to be the source of all this wrongdoing – it is he who gets us to do what we shouldn't do. He is the source of evil. But we have to be careful not to allow popular fantasy to distort the truth. There may be spiritual forces that oppose the way God would want things to be, but in the end Christians believe that such forces will always be defeated by the power of God's goodness and his love. In the Bible, the person of Satan is not so much the source of all wickedness as the one who is the great Tempter. In the Genesis story, the snake tempted Eve to eat the apple. In the story of Job, Satan was allowed to make Job suffer in order to tempt him to curse God. In the wilderness, Satan tempted Jesus to use power for his own selfish reasons. It was later traditions and works such as Milton's *Paradise Lost* that helped create the more dramatic idea of the wicked devil.

Religions have always been a key way to help people understand and manage the complexities that arise from the mixture of good and evil. The key Christian understanding does not underestimate either but is convinced that the good will ultimately win. Where human choice is responsible for bad things happening, God and we can transform the situation through forgiveness and by seeking to make amends. Where the world of nature produces bad effects, we are called upon to seek answers using the gifts God gives us – reduction of greenhouse gases, creation of flood defences, research into disease. It is in facing creatively both the delight of what is good and the pain of what is wrong that we grow as human beings.

CHAPTER 12

Miracles

It's a matter of belief

Miracles are unusual! They do not happen very often. But it is not just their rarity that makes them miraculous. Eclipses of the sun are quite rare but we do not these days consider them to be miraculous, although they would have been considered to be at one time. In the Bible, eclipses were considered to be the result of a direct intervention by God. We know now that they are natural events that can be explained scientifically. Miracles aren't: they do not comply with our scientific understanding. For some people, that strengthens their belief in miracles. Other people conclude that there are no such things as miracles – other explanations must be possible.

As in the case of the eclipse, events once understood as miracles may, as the result of advances in our knowledge, be seen to be quite normal, although perhaps unusual. Jesus gained a considerable reputation as a preacher but more especially as a healer and an exorcist. His healings are often described as examples of the miracles he performed, indicating the presence of God's power at work in him or indeed as 'proof' of his divinity.

Signs

In John's Gospel Jesus' miracles are described as 'signs'. John was especially interested in indicating the reaction people had to these 'signs' – whether they led to faith or rejection. Such healing miracles were also seen, by St Mark for example, as a sign that Jesus was involved in a battle with evil. Illness was understood to be a sign of the presence of evil, or indeed as the direct influence of demons and spirits. There was not the same sharp distinction in those days between what we would call 'healings' and 'exorcisms'. The rather dramatic symptoms of epilepsy, for example, led to the belief that a person suffering from epileptic seizures was in the power of an evil spirit. In 'casting out' the spirit, Jesus cured the epilepsy.

Healing

Some of those who came to Jesus for healing might be considered these days as suffering from mental illness or psychosomatic illnesses – for example, a deep sense of guilt that had resulted in a paralysis. Jesus' insight into a person's inner being enabled him to release the sufferer from their mental/spiritual torment and therefore 'cure' their physical condition.

Just how many of the reported miracles can be explained in this way is difficult to know because the events have not been recorded in those terms. Our increased knowledge of the way the mind can affect the body means that a number of apparently physical conditions may be psychosomatic and that their 'cure' would not necessarily involve physical (or 'divine') help.

Resurrection

But such explanations do not cover all the reported miracles. There is no reason to suggest that the widow's son or Lazarus were not really dead (Luke 7:11-17; John 11:1-44). They weren't simply in a coma or a catatonic state from which Jesus roused them. These events were recorded as evidence of Jesus' power over the evil of death and as signs of 'resurrection'.

Jesus' own resurrection was clearly understood as miraculous. It was evidence of God's action (God raised Jesus), vindicating all that Jesus had done and revealing his power over death. There is no evidence for the naturalistic explanations that have been put forward, such as 'the body was stolen', 'he wasn't really dead', or that the belief in his return to life was a piece of mass hysteria on the part of the disciples. People either believe in the resurrection as an event that is mysterious and only explainable in terms of God's action or not.

As far as their own 'life beyond death' is concerned, many Christians find comfort in the promise Jesus made to his disciples that he was going to prepare a place for them (John 14:2, 3), that where he was going they would be also. Some Christians interpret this to mean being with God rather than simply being in a location.

Nature miracles

Other miracles, such as the 'nature' miracles when Jesus walked on water, stilled a storm or turned water into wine, have been given naturalistic explanations which may or may not satisfy the sceptic. For the Gospel writers, the ability to control storms or defy the normal laws of nature was part of God's power – nature was in his control. Jesus' miracles therefore gave support to their belief that not only was God working through Jesus but also that he was himself divine. The real interest is not so much in the details of the events themselves as what could be learnt from them.

This, for example, is John's purpose in recording the miracle (the sign) of the changing of water into wine at the wedding in Cana. Our interest is in what actually happened. John's interest is much more in what it meant. For John it showed how the old Jewish traditions with their purification rites were giving way to a new, fuller way that Jesus was introducing – as different from the old as wine is to water.

Miracles continue to interest people. For the Roman Catholic Church, miraculous healings through a person's action or mediation is part of the test for them to be declared a saint. People continue to believe that in healing services and through the power of prayer they witness God at work in miracles (see 'Healing' in chapter 15). Sceptics will always cast doubt on their existence. Believers find in them a source of faith or, at the very least, evidence of the complex and mysterious way God's world can work that is not always capable of a scientific explanation.

Heaven and hell

Going up, going down

Heaven and hell have both had a bad press. Those who think that the Christian religion is all wishful thinking and a way of compensating for the misfortunes of this life talk of heaven as 'pie in the sky when you die'. And hell is seen as the place of punishment, filled with victims by a sadistic God. It has to be admitted that some Christian writing and art has only helped to reinforce this impression: a marriage may have been 'made in heaven' and too many people have experienced holidays 'from hell'. Twanging harps on damp clouds and screaming from endless torture may be the popular view, but they hardly convey what heaven and hell are about.

Above

In traditional ancient cosmology the sky was a tent or a dome covering the Earth and the heavens were either identified with the sky or a place beyond the sky. The Bible sometimes talks of heaven being where God is, although more often he is said to reside above the heavens. In the New Testament Jesus is said to have looked up to heaven in prayer (Mark 6:41), and in the account of his final departure from his disciples he was said to have been 'taken up . . . into heaven' (Acts 1:11). From that time onward he was believed to be with the Father in heaven.

Modern cosmology has presented us with a very different view of the universe, and the first Russian astronaut, Yuri Gagarin, was able confidently to report that there was no God when he rocketed above the sky.

Below

If heaven was pictured as being above us, then hell was clearly below – the nether regions. When the Earth was believed to be a flat disc, hell was not at the centre of our globe but somewhere beneath us. Medieval Christian spirituality and art did much to provide a picture of hell as a place of fire and brimstone, torment and torture. They built on imagery that is to be found in books like the Revelation of St John the Divine, the last book of the Bible. Medieval wall paintings of the judgement by God of men and women, called Doom paintings, can still be seen in some churches. They helped to present the vivid contrast of the hell suffered by those who were evil or who rejected God and the bliss enjoyed by the faithful. Such pictures of hell had something of the style of the video nasty about them; they were purposely violent in order to be a deterrent to wrongdoing.

People believed in heaven and hell as actual places, and some Christians still do, even though they are not sure exactly where to set them. But where heaven and hell are is less important than what they represent. John Paul Sartre, the French writer, said that 'Hell was other people'. They are more to do with relationship and state than with place.

Final resurrection

People often talk about meeting their husband or wife, their children and friends when they get to heaven. They find it a great comfort to think that this will be so. It of course assumes that we will be in a state that will make recognition possible. That we do not lose our individuality after death, as some religions believe, is very important in the Christian understanding. Christians do not believe that we are somehow 'absorbed' into a general state of being or that we are reincarnated for a further period on Earth.

St Paul talks about the body that we shall have after death being not like our earthly body but a spiritual body (1 Corinthians 15:35-54). In Catholic theology it is believed that our 'soul and body' shall only be reunited at the final resurrection and not immediately after death.

If to be loved perfectly really is heavenly, then to be loved by God and to be in the presence of that perfect loving relationship is heaven. Being kept from that loving relationship might be described as hell. On such an understanding, heaven is to be in the presence of God and hell is to be absent from God.

In the presence of God

Or it might be that heaven and hell are both states experienced in the presence of God. For those who know God to be a loving Father and who freely love God in response, existence is heavenly. To be in the presence of God but unable to see his love and respond to it might be hellish.

According to such a view, it is not that God sends people either to heaven or hell but that we decide it by our own choices. Those who are utterly self-absorbed are unable to respond to God and to others with outgoing love, and to live like that is to live in hell, although they may never realise it. Only those who enjoy outgoing, self-giving, loving relationships can see that in comparison with the way things are for them, self-centredness is hell. In Catholic theology, being able to enter the divine presence or to have the joy of seeing God directly ('the beatific vision') is only possible after we have been through a process of 'purging' to prepare us – this lies behind the teaching about 'purgatory'.

People question whether a loving, forgiving God could ever condemn someone to hell for all eternity. For some, this merely reflects taking seriously the evil that some people are capable of during their lives and the punishment they deserve. For victims of evil it can be seen as a righting of wrongs, an appropriate justice perhaps denied them while alive. Others would argue that God's forgiveness and love are always on offer – for everyone, now and eternally. What matters is whether or not we take up the offer.

It has to be admitted that most of the talk about heaven and hell, where they are, what they are like and what goes on in them is a matter of speculation, and sometimes of fantasy. What the Christian seeks to do is to speak of them only in relation to all else that is known about God through Jesus.

CHAPTER 14

Sin and forgiveness

I'm not very holy

Christians strive to be 'good', by which is meant they seek to live following the example of Jesus and in line with the will of God. But every Christian knows that there are times when they fail. They say and do things that are wrong. That doesn't mean that they are being hypocrites, unless of course they make out that they always tell the truth and then deliberately lie, for example. In common with all human beings, Christians are sinners. What they do claim, however, is that through the love of God as shown in the death and resurrection of Jesus, they are forgiven sinners. And that makes all the difference.

What is sin?

So are wrongdoing and sinning the same thing? Above all things, sin is to do with our relationship with God. The Bible suggests that none of us gets that entirely right. Indeed, it is part of the human condition that all human beings get it wrong. That is part of what the story of Adam's disobedience (the account of the Fall in Genesis 3) is seeking to teach. There is a kind of bias built into us that makes us go against what is right, breaking what should be a perfect relationship of loving obedience towards God.

Missing the mark

On the basis of that broken relationship, sin is understood as doing, saying and thinking things which fall short of what God wants and expects of us. It's 'missing the mark' of what we are called to do

73

and be. We do not always hit the bull's eye. We are called to be truthful, and we aim to be truthful, but there are times when we miss the mark: we lie, we sin. It is sin because it is against what is understood to be God's will for human beings. In formal terms, it is against what God commands, against his rules. The most obvious of those rules are what are called the Ten Commandments (Deuteronomy 5:6-21) and they include things like not worshipping idols, not committing murder or adultery, not stealing, honouring parents. In the Old Testament there are hundreds of rules. Little wonder people broke some of them.

Two rules

Jesus summed up all the rules in just two: Love God; love your neighbour (other people). If we were perfectly loving, all would be well. But we aren't; no one is. It's the way we are, although that doesn't excuse us from the moral and spiritual duty to do things right. Some see it as a genetic matter, derived from our evolution, part of the necessary 'selfishness' that ensures our survival. The Christian view sees it as a spiritual matter – a matter of our relationship with God from which all else flows. We want our own way, rather than God's way. We think we know better. We sin because we are sinners, i.e. missers of the mark in our love of God and in our love for others. That doesn't mean that we never do loving things or never do what God wants. There is true goodness and unselfish loving action, but it is never perfect. We can do our best to make amends but, at the end of the day, we can never do enough.

This sounds like a very pessimistic view of humanity, and it is made worse by the fact that Christians believe God does not collude with our wrongdoing. He does not ignore our failure to love him and others fully. The Bible makes it quite clear – wrongdoing means punishment; sin means that the broken relationship with

God is to be judged. Because God is holy, he cannot ignore what is wrong. All have sinned; all are for the high jump!

That would be a very dark prospect indeed. But what Christianity believes and wants to share with everyone is that there is good news. What we cannot do for ourselves God has done for us. We cannot restore the loving relationship with God, but God can restore his loving relationship with us. He can and he has – it's just up to us to grasp it.

New relationship

God offers us not just forgiveness for the things we do wrong and for the failure to do good things, but he also offers us a new relationship that is stronger than anything we can do to break it. He has shown this through the life, death and resurrection of Jesus. Jesus, it is believed, was the one human being whose loving relationship with God and others was not broken. He was fully and unselfishly loving. In spite of everything bad that people did to him – misunderstand him, betray him, desert him, torture him, cruelly kill him – he kept on loving them, forgiving them. Here was the love of God in action, demonstrated in human terms. In Jesus, God, as it were, gave himself away (sacrificed himself) to show his love and his forgiveness. The cost of such love was all-encompassing; it involved death. Had that been the end, then hatred and selfishness and not love would have had the final say. But the resurrection of Jesus proved that it was not in vain. Love is the winner; forgiveness does prevail.

God made possible what we could not do. He restores what we break; he forgives what we spoil. This is not cheap forgiveness – the death on the cross showed how costly it is. It is not inevitable forgiveness – it is offered, but we have to receive it and respond to it. All we have to do is accept it – there are no other conditions – and it is offered to everyone. We do not have to be holy to be loved and forgiven. But as people who are loved and forgiven by God, we can strive to be holy (unselfishly loving).

Hope

The Christian view about the human condition is not in the end pessimistic – it is realistic and full of hope. It is realistic because it takes seriously the fact that we all get things wrong. It is full of hope because our future depends not on what we do but on what God has done and does with us.

CHAPTER 15

Worship and church services
What's on the menu?

Human beings have found innumerable ways of expressing their sense of 'the other' in acts of worship: from lighting candles to making burnt offerings; from throwing locks of hair into a river to sharing a meal; from singing to dancing; from shouting to sitting in silence. There is almost no limit to what imagination and spiritual sensitivity have come up with, from the sophisticated and formal to the spontaneous and restless. Different religions each have their own particular culture of worship, and variations within that.

Christians may be clear that they are offering worship to the God who is known as Father, and they do this through Jesus Christ, the Son, and in the power of the Holy Spirit, but how they worship and what their worship includes varies greatly. There are, however, some general strands.

Liturgical

One broad distinction is between liturgical and non-liturgical worship. Liturgical worship follows a set order, moving in a largely predetermined way from one section to the next. Collections of liturgical texts may be gathered together, e.g. the Roman Catholic *Missal* and *Breviary* or the Church of England's *Book of Common Prayer* and *Common Worship*. As well as services for particular occasions such as baptisms, weddings or funerals, such books provide services that focus on readings from the Bible, the psalms, canticles (sacred songs from other parts of the Bible), prayers and a sermon. The most important liturgical service is the Mass or Holy Communion.

Liturgical worship has the advantage that regular worshippers know what to expect. It provides an orderly act of worship whose shape and content is not dependent upon the liturgical ability of the worship leader. But for some worshippers it can appear over formal and very conservative with comparatively little active participation by the congregation.

Non-liturgical

Non-liturgical services are not based on a prescribed form of worship, although many have a recognisable pattern of praise, thanksgiving, confession and intercession with biblical readings and a sermon or address. Hymns and worship songs feature strongly. Such services are more spontaneous, more participatory. They are felt to be more accessible than much liturgical worship and are often associated with free and Pentecostal churches.

Family worship

Worship has often been seen as primarily an adult activity. Children were taken to church, but unless there was a specific 'Children's Service', little attempt was made, or even thought to be necessary, to engage and involve them. More recently, partly due to a better understanding of children's spirituality and also because there is a concern to attract youngsters and young families, church leaders have looked for ways to make worship more 'child friendly'. Sunday schools have tended to give way to events in the week that, while having a religious content, have more of the atmosphere of a club. The worship is informal, engaging and participatory.

Concerned that families should come together for worship, efforts have been made either to provide **all-age worship** or, in the case of Eucharistic worship, to have part of the service time spent separately but then to bring everyone together for the central act of

Communion when those who are not confirmed or in full membership receive a blessing rather than the bread and wine.

Jesus' instruction

As a Jew, the worship Jesus was familiar with was the worship of the synagogue and the Temple. While he gave some instructions on how his followers should pray (Matthew 6), he said little about the content of worship. Yet one highly significant instruction he did give has been the foundation of the most central of Christian acts of worship. At the last meal he had with his friends on the night before his death, he took bread, gave thanks, broke it and shared it with his disciples. At the end of the meal he took a cup of wine and gave thanks, and it too was shared by his followers. He told them to do this as a way of remembering him – the bread as a symbol of his body that would be broken on the cross; the wine reminding them of his spilt blood. It became the focal point of what is variously known as the **Mass, Holy Communion,** the **Lord's Supper** or the **Eucharist** (Thanksgiving). At this service, Christians join together in what is a symbolic meal in which they strengthen their relationship (their communion) with one another and also with God and God with them.

Sacrament or symbol

Exactly what is happening at this service is ultimately a mystery, the work of God's Spirit feeding the spirits of the worshippers. Again, there are broadly two distinct ways of understanding this: a sacramental view and a symbolic view. Both believe that what happens is the work of God and is beneficial to the spiritual life of the worshippers. It is an act of God's 'grace' made available through the sacrifice of Jesus on the cross which is 'shown forth' or remembered at this service.

The 'sacramental' view understands that in some way God, through the action of the priest (consecration), changes the bread and wine so they become the very means of God's saving and nurturing activity for the believer. In traditional Roman Catholic understanding, the bread and wine 'become' the body and blood of Jesus. The very substance of the bread and wine change. This is what has been called 'transubstantiation'. A slightly different view says that the substance doesn't change but what the bread and wine signify does change, from physical food and drink to the spiritual 'food' of Jesus' body and blood, offering to worshippers all the benefits of what Jesus' death and resurrection achieved in terms of forgiveness and new life.

More evangelical or protestant worshippers do not believe that the bread and wine change but that they remain simply bread and wine, and that in the context of this particular act of worship they are symbols of Jesus' saving love. The worshippers benefit from this through their faith in Jesus, which is strengthened as they receive the bread and wine.

The word

In the Eucharistic service the emphasis is on what God is doing for and in the spiritual life of the worshippers through the 'sacrament/symbol' of the bread and wine. Other worship puts more emphasis on what God is doing through the word of God – the Bible and the sermon. These might be categorised as **Services of the Word**. In traditional form they are services like Matins and Evensong which have their origins in the round of daily worship offered by monks and nuns. The focus lies upon what is read and said. Such acts of worship are understood to be God's way of feeding, challenging and comforting worshippers through the words of the Bible (God's word) and the words of prayers and hymns and, especially, the sermon, preached 'in the name of God'.

Praise, confession and intercession

Worship is basically about our relationship with God and his with us. Much of what has been described so far has concentrated on what God does for and in us through worship. But worship also has much to do with what we bring to God, how we show our love for God, our thanks for all he gives us, the requests we bring for ourselves and for his world and for other people.

The sheer joy and wonder of knowing God and wanting to speak or sing about his greatness, his majesty, his glory is an essential part of worship and is the focus of services of **praise**. While in such services praise will be the central feature, it will normally feature in any service. It is part of what worship means – giving God his 'worth'. Similarly, because God is holy, worshippers do not assume that they can come to worship – enter his presence, as it were – without acknowledging that they are not 'worthy'. Most services will therefore include an act of **confession**, where we admit what we have done wrong or the good we have failed to do, and ask for God's forgiveness.

Worshippers properly concentrate on God – what he does, what he promises, what he commands – but they do not (or should not) leave the world entirely behind when worshipping. Worship is not an act of escapism. Because all the world is under God's care – both the physical environment and all the people of the world – worshippers bring their concerns to God for that world and for people who are in particular need. So there are prayers that not only speak of God but also of those concerns. These are the **intercessions** and will usually include prayers for the world and its peace, for the Church and its leaders, for the local community, and for individuals who have particular needs.

Healing

Some acts of worship have a particular focus on the needs of those who are ill or troubled, anxious or guilty – in other words, those who are sick or broken in spirit. Such services are **healing** services at which worshippers are reminded of the healing power of God through his spirit. In various ways, sometimes very dramatically, they call upon God's spirit to bring healing to those for whom there is a special concern. Such services may include the 'laying-on of hands' when the worship leader or a person who is understood to have a particular gift for healing prays with and for a person, lays hands on them and calls upon God to heal whatever is amiss in the person's life. This may not only be a physical illness but might be some other kind of dis-ease. In some traditions this may be accompanied by the anointing of the person with holy oil. Anointing and laying-on of hands have a long history in both Judaism and Christianity.

Specific services

Because worship involves our relationship with God, and because he is concerned with the whole of us and our lives, there is nothing that cannot potentially be brought into worship or be the focus for worship. Particular activities such as education, particular people such as prisoners, or particular events such as harvest can all be the focus for worship. There are services for fishermen, for the armed services, for pets and for ramblers, for civic occasions and for music festivals. In churches that follow the Church's calendar, the services will reflect the feasts and festivals that the calendar provides (see chapter 16 – 'Feasts and festivals'). Personal occasions may also be marked by an act of worship – births and baptisms, marriages and anniversaries, funerals and acts of remembrance.

Feasts and festivals

Days of celebration

Just as families celebrate birthdays, anniversaries and special events, so too does the Christian Church – events that are very significant in the story of Jesus and in the history and life of faith. Although Christmas and Easter are celebrated by all Christian churches, it will largely depend on the particular denomination as to which of the other festivals and feasts are observed.

Feasts and festivals recalling events in the life of Jesus

Christmas

This is the day when Christians celebrate the birth of Jesus (Matthew 1:18–2:23; Luke 2:1-20). It is traditionally observed on 25 December, although there is no basis in the Bible for choosing this date.

In the early Church there was considerable speculation about the actual date, and at one time a date in May was suggested. The December date was first known to have been used in the year 336. It is thought that this date was chosen as a way of countering the celebration of the birth of 'the victorious sun' as advocated by Mithraism, an ancient pagan religion. The Christians saw this day as celebrating not the birth of the sun but the birth of the 'Sun of righteousness' (Malachi 4:2). The choice of 25 December spread from Rome throughout the western part of Christendom. In the East, 6 January was a day of celebrating Jesus' baptism as well as the visit of the wise men (see 'Epiphany' below) and was initially more important than Jesus' birth. By the middle of the fifth century, East and West were celebrating Jesus' birth on 25 December, apart from the Armenian Church which still celebrates Christ's birth on 6 January.

The joyful celebration has popularly been marked by festivities and merrymaking – a legacy of the pagan Roman festivals it replaced. Many of the current customs, such as decorated trees and Christmas cards, are in fact largely Victorian introductions and show the influence of the Queen's German Consort, Prince Albert.

The day following Christmas Day is commonly called Boxing Day. In the Church it is the day when St Stephen, the first Christian martyr, is remembered. Metal boxes would be put out to collect money for the poor on this day. From medieval times it was the practice on this day to give servants and tradespeople a boxed gift, and this may be the origin of the day's name.

On 27 December the Church remembers the young children of Bethlehem who were slaughtered on the orders of King Herod in a vain attempt to kill the infant Jesus. The event is recorded in Matthew 2:16-18 and is known as the Feast of the Holy Innocents.

Epiphany

Since the fourth century, this festival, held on 6 January, has in the West recalled the visit of the wise men to the infant Jesus (Matthew 2:1-15).

The word 'epiphany' means 'manifestation' or 'showing forth'. This was originally associated with the baptism of Jesus by John which marked the beginning of Jesus' public ministry. However, the visit of the wise men was also seen as a 'manifestation' since it was understood as the time when the infant Christ was 'shown forth' to the non-Jewish world as represented by the foreign wise men who had come from the East. The day marks Twelfth Night which has traditionally been a time of dramatic performances and music (mumming and wassailing) and when the Christmas decorations are taken down.

Ash Wednesday

This day marks the beginning of the season of Lent when Christians remember the 40 days Jesus spent in the wilderness fasting and being tempted (Matthew 4:1-11; Mark 1:12, 13; Luke 4:1-13). It has no fixed date because it is linked to Easter, the date of which is determined by the phases of the moon.

Lent is a time of fasting and penance, and this has traditionally been marked on Ash Wednesday by the practice of marking the foreheads of worshippers with ashes made by burning the palm crosses of the previous year. Ashes symbolise mourning and penitence.

The day before Ash Wednesday is known as Shrove Tuesday – now more commonly known in Britain as Pancake Tuesday when pancakes are cooked and pancake races are held. Shrove comes from the act of 'shriving', i.e. confession and absolution, which occurred on this day. In some cultures, for example in New Orleans, the period leading up to Lent is known as Mardi Gras. It is a time of festivities culminating in 'Fat Tuesday' (Mardi Gras) when people eat rich foods prior to the start of the Lenten season of fast.

Mothering Sunday

This is the fourth Sunday in Lent and is also known as 'Refreshment Sunday' or 'Laetare Sunday' (which comes from the first word in Latin of the Introit for the Mass on that day: 'Rejoice with Jerusalem . . .' Isaiah 66:10). At this mid-point in Lent some relaxation of the traditional penitential observances is allowed – hence the name 'refreshment'.

The origins of the name 'Mothering Sunday' have been associated with various customs, such as mothers being visited on this day, visits made to the cathedral (mother church of the dioceses), or words from the traditional reading from the epistle for this day which includes the words 'Jerusalem . . . is our mother' (Galatians 4:26). In many churches the day is marked by children presenting gifts of flowers to their mothers, and sermons focusing on the theme of mothers – either our own mothers, the act of mothering, Mother Church or Mary, mother of Jesus.

Father's Day is increasingly and variously celebrated, most often on the third Sunday of June.

Palm Sunday

This day, at the beginning of Holy Week, recalls the triumphal entry of Jesus into Jerusalem, riding on a donkey (Matthew 21:1-11; Mark 11:1-11; Luke 19:29-40; John 12:12-19). The crowds welcomed him as king, waved palm branches and laid their coats in the road. The blessing of palm branches or palm crosses, and processions mark the day.

In the Middle Ages worshippers would process from one church to another where the palms were blessed and distributed. A representation of Christ – a cross, a Bible or a carved figure – was often set on a wooden donkey and carried in the procession. These days it is not unusual to have a live donkey in the procession. A highly elaborate ceremony for the blessing of the palms was developed in the early Middle Ages in England but it was rejected by Order of Council in 1549 and was never included in the *Book of Common Prayer*. In 1955 the liturgies of Holy Week in the Roman Catholic Church were revised, and this ceremony was radically simplified.

Holy Week

This is the week that leads up to Easter and is traditionally observed as a week of devotion to the Passion of Christ. Churches may hold a daily service (commonly an evening service called Compline) in which the events of the week are particularly recalled.

Maundy Thursday (also known as Holy Thursday)

This is the Thursday of Holy Week when Christians recall the occasion when Jesus had a last meal with his disciples before his crucifixion the next day (Good Friday) (Matthew 26:17-35; Mark 14:12-25; Luke 22:7-38; John 13-17). An evening service of Holy Communion is normally held, during which the minister may wash the feet of representatives of the congregation. In some churches the service concludes with the stripping of the altar, the procession of the reserved sacrament when the consecrated bread and wine are carried in procession from the main altar to a side chapel, and a vigil that recalls the time Jesus spent in prayer in the Garden of Gethsemane prior to his arrest.

The name 'Maundy' probably comes from the Latin *mandatum* (commandment) and is the opening word of the phrase, 'I give you a new commandment, that you love one another.' Jesus used these words when explaining to his disciples why, at the meal, he had stripped off and taken the position of a slave and washed their feet (John 13). An alternative explanation has been suggested that relates to the traditional ceremony whereby the British monarch distributed money to the poor. An English word 'maund' meant 'to beg'. The Maundy money ceremony still occurs in the Church of England, taking place these days in a different church (usually a cathedral) each year. It is no longer the poor but representatives of the local elderly who receive the 'Royal Maundy', and the specially minted small silver coins are tokens of the alms originally distributed.

Good Friday

This day recalls the death of Jesus on the cross (Matthew 27; Mark 15; Luke 23; John 19). In the Catholic tradition it is a day of fasting and devotion, although in some Protestant churches it is a day of celebration. Good Friday and Holy Saturday are the only days of the year when, in the Roman Catholic Church, the Mass (Holy Communion) is not celebrated.

A common pattern of devotion that has developed alongside other liturgical provision is that of the Three Hours service, held between noon and 3pm. It was first introduced by the Jesuits after the time of the Reformation and has most widely been adopted by the Church of England. The Stations of the Cross, usually 14 carvings or pictures depicting the incidents of Jesus' last journey from Pilate's house to his entombment and which hang on the walls of some churches, may be used as the focus of prayer and devotions as worshippers walk from station to station.

It is also quite common these days for churches to organise a 'Procession of Witness' on Good Friday morning in which the faithful process through the town or village carrying a large cross and bearing witness to the crucifixion of Christ. In some places these have become elaborate re-enactments, with costumed individuals taking the parts of the main characters in the events of the day.

Holy Saturday (or Easter Even)

This commemorates the resting of Jesus' body in the tomb between his death on Good Friday and the resurrection on Easter Day. It is not usual for Holy Communion to be celebrated on this day, and the day's ceremonies normally take place during the night of Saturday–Sunday. An all-night vigil of prayer has been traditional since the time of the early Church.

The Paschal Vigil is the first of the Easter Services. Traditionally it is held between sunset on the Saturday and dawn on Easter Day and was when people were baptised and received their first Communion. From a newly created fire, the Paschal Candle (a large candle representing the risen Christ as light of the world) is lit before it is processed through the church where candles held by members of the congregation are also lit as the proclamation 'The Light of Christ' is said or sung. There is then a service of readings, followed by baptisms or the renewal of baptismal vows and a service of Holy Communion. The exact format of the service can vary considerably according to a church's tradition. Sometimes the service of the new fire and Paschal Candle are held at dawn.

Easter Day

Easter Day celebrates the resurrection of Christ and is the greatest of the festivals, though it is less significant than Christmas in popular culture. Its date is not fixed. It is the first Sunday after the full moon following the March equinox and can vary between 22 March and 25 April. Because the traditional way of calculation understood a day to begin at sunset, the first celebrations of Easter may begin during the night of Holy Saturday and Easter Sunday (see 'Holy Saturday' above).

The events of Easter Day are recorded in all four of the Gospels but in differing forms and with different emphases (Matthew 28; Mark 16; Luke 24; John 20). The Gospels do not describe the actual resurrection but record the appearances of Jesus to various of his disciples in the garden, the upper room and by the seashore. They seek to establish that it was a 'real' event, not a piece of wishful thinking; that it was the same Jesus, not a substitute; that he had a bodily form but it was not limited by the normal conditions of the physical body (he appeared through closed doors yet ate with his disciples). There was both continuity and change, and not everyone believed. His appearances lasted over a period of some 40 days.

Because the first resurrection events occurred in a garden, some churches create small gardens depicting the tomb with the stone rolled away, the empty cross, and flowers symbolising the new life. It is this same symbolism that is to be found in Easter eggs – the shell symbolises the tomb and the chick the emerging new life.

Ascension Day

This day marks the end of the 40 days during which the risen Christ appeared to his disciples (Acts 1:3-11). Jesus withdrew into heaven, witnessed by his disciples. This is said to have occurred on the Mount of Olives, and guides still show marks in the stone that they say are the imprint of Jesus' feet as he ascended to heaven. It is not possible to know what actually happened, and in Luke's Gospel the event occurs at Bethany on the night of the resurrection itself (Luke 24:50-3). Theologically, the accounts seek to convey the truth that Jesus is now at the right hand of God in glory and to make a break between the time when he was physically present on Earth and his departure which led to the gift of the Holy Spirit to assure believers of his continuing spiritual presence with them.

Whit Sunday (Pentecost)

The account in Acts (Acts 2:1-13) tells of the disciples all being together on the day of Pentecost. Pentecost was a Jewish festival when the first fruits of the corn harvest were presented, and later commemorated the giving of the Law to Moses. In the Christian tradition it is associated with the gift of the Holy Spirit who descended on the disciples like tongues of fire. The event is also associated with the ability to speak in tongues, on this occasion in languages from all around the known world. It is generally understood to be the birthday of the Church and the start of its mission to take the gospel to all corners of the Earth.

Trinity Sunday

This is not a feast celebrating a part of the story of Jesus but a day on which the distinctive Christian doctrine concerning the nature of God is celebrated, and to that extent concludes the round of 'Jesus festivals'. The celebration of this day, a week after Whit Sunday, dates back to the Middle Ages.

The doctrine of the Holy Trinity asserts that in his very nature God is three 'persons' – Father, Son and Holy Spirit – but that the three are one. It is a way of seeking to understand the mystery of God understood in terms of relationship between God as Creator, God as Redeemer and God as Sustainer.

Transfiguration

Transfiguration is celebrated on 6 August and recalls the occasion when Jesus, accompanied by three of his disciples – Peter, James and John – appeared in his divine glory on the Mount of the Transfiguration – possibly Tabor or Hermon (Matthew 17:1-13; Mark 9:2-13; Luke 9:28-36). During the event, Moses and Elijah appeared with Jesus, indicating that his status as Messiah, the 'anointed one', was testified to by both the Law and the prophets. A voice was heard, similar to the one at his baptism, declaring Jesus to be God's son.

Other feasts and festivals

A number of festivals, celebrated particularly in the Roman Catholic Church, focus on the Blessed Virgin Mary.

The Immaculate Conception (8 December)

A festival to celebrate the conception of the Blessed Virgin Mary has been observed since the seventh century, and in 1854 Pope Pius IX pronounced that Mary had been kept free from all stain of original sin from the first moment of her conception. The doctrine drew upon teaching going back to the early Fathers of the Church and is said to have biblical foundation in Genesis 3:15 and Luke 1:28. Although the belief was widely contested in the medieval period, it was formally declared as part of Catholic teaching by the Council of Trent and has generally been accepted in the Roman Catholic Church since the sixteenth century.

The Annunciation (25 March)

Luke tells us of the visit of the angel Gabriel to Mary, announcing that she is to conceive through the agency of the Holy Spirit and will be the mother of Jesus (Luke 1:26-38). Its celebration on this day was not widely agreed until the eighth century and required the fixing of the date for Christmas. Since it occurs in Lent it was excluded from the ban on feasts during Lent. In Spain it was celebrated on 18 December in order to avoid it being celebrated during Lent.

The Assumption (15 August)

The belief that Mary did not die but that at the end of her life was assumed, body and soul, into heaven was unknown in the early Church and was not formulated until the end of the sixth century. It became widely celebrated in the West from the eighth century onwards, but it was not until 1950 that Pope Pius XII, after decades of pressure, defined the doctrine (in *Munificentissimus Deus*).

Harvest festivals

In the worship of the Church of England these are among the most popular Church festivals, especially in rural areas. They reflect a long tradition of communal acts of thanksgiving for the harvest and the bounty of the Earth that certainly stretches back to Old Testament times and are to be found in many cultures and religions. In medieval England, Lammas Day (1 August) was commonly recognised as a day for thanksgiving for the 'first fruits', and bread baked from the new wheat was solemnly blessed. The present-day customs date back to the revival of this practice by the Revd R.

Hawker at Morwenstone in Cornwall in 1843. The gifts of fruit and vegetables are traditionally distributed to the poor, although these days they will often include tinned and packet food. In fishing areas, a Festival of the Sea may also be celebrated.

The saints

Both the Roman Catholic Church and the Church of England have calendars of saints' days when various saints and leading Church figures are remembered as examples of godly living and faithful Christian action. In the liturgy for the day there are appropriate readings from Scripture and Collects.

Devotion to the saints, including the belief that the saintly dead make intercessions on behalf of the living, is given scriptural basis in the implications of St Paul's teaching on the 'body of Christ' (Romans 12:4-8; Ephesians 2:19). Liturgical expression followed popular devotion to the saints from the fourth century onwards.

Church Councils attempted to curb the increasing use of legendary material and superstitious excesses surrounding the lives of the saints, and the Reformed Churches roundly condemned the practice of praying to the saints. In the Thirty-nine Articles of the Church of England it is viewed as 'a fond thing vainly invented', and the practice was only reintroduced in the Victorian period by the high wing of the Church.

All Saints and All Souls

The Church has long wanted to honour its saints – the unknown ones as well as those who are famous. Since the seventh century, a day has been set aside for this general devotion. Originally it was 13 May. In the eighth century, Pope Gregory III dedicated a chapel in the basilica of St Peter in Rome to 'All the Saints' on 1 November, and Gregory IV ordered that it should be this day when the saints would be remembered.

The virtuous and well-respected Odio, Abbott of Cluny (963–1048), established the practice at Cluny of observing 2 November as a day for commemorating the faithful departed – All Souls' Day. The practice soon expanded to the whole of the Western Church. In the Catholic tradition, a distinction is made between the saints, who are those believed to have acquired the vision of God in heaven (the ultimate destiny of believers), and those who have died but have not yet reached this state of purification. In other traditions, 'saints' means all the faithful people of God, living and dead.

During the season of All Saints and All Souls, many churches hold services in which worshippers have the opportunity to specifically remember those from among their family and friends who have died. Relatives of those who have died in the previous twelve months are especially invited. In hospitals where there is a maternity unit, chaplains may hold services to which parents are invited to remember babies who have died either as aborted foetuses, still-births or neonatally.

All Saints' Day is also known as All Hallows, and the evening before is celebrated in popular culture as Hallowe'en ('All Hallows' evening'). Whether or not this had a pagan Celtic origin is uncertain, but it has come to be associated with various practices such as 'trick or treat', bonfires and apple-bobbing, which may well have their origins and festivities associated with the dead.

Remembrance Sunday

In the United Kingdom, the second Sunday in November is the occasion when the nation remembers those who died in the two World Wars and in conflicts since. It is the Sunday closest to 11 November – the day in 1918 when at 11am hostilities ceased with the signing of the Armistice. Services on this day are often held not only in churches but also at war memorials.

In London, the national act of remembrance is led by the monarch in a ceremony at the Cenotaph. The red poppy is the symbol of this day, recalling the poppies in the killing fields of Flanders and now sold in aid of the British Legion funds that go towards the care of members of the armed services and their relatives.

CHAPTER 17

Who's who in the church
Some titles and roles

For people who haven't been involved with the church, and even for those who have attended for many years, the names of the various officers and leaders can be a mystery and very confusing.

Here is a list to help sort some of them out.

Archbishop

An archbishop is a bishop (see 'Bishop') of senior rank. Most usually an archbishop will have responsibility over a number of dioceses (ecclesiastical areas each with their own bishop) that in the Anglican Communion are collectively known as a Province. In the Church of England there are two Provinces – Canterbury and York – each with their own Archbishop. The Archbishop of Canterbury is the more senior of the two. In the Roman Catholic Church the leader of such a grouping of dioceses is called a Metropolitan Archbishop.

Archdeacon

An archdeacon was originally the senior deacon (see 'Deacon'), often with responsibility for the finances of a bishop and diocese. Next in seniority to the bishop, an archdeacon was later required to be a priest and had responsibility for an area of a diocese known as an archdeaconry. Although a significant role in the Catholic Church during the High Middle Ages, the title has now largely fallen out of use in that Church and the responsibilities have been taken up by other officers.

Bishop

A bishop is the third and most senior of the three traditional forms of ordained ministry: deacon, priest and bishop. A bishop normally has responsibility for leadership of a diocese (an ecclesiastical area) as preacher and teacher of the faith, for having care of the clergy and for being the focus of unity in the church. In a large diocese, a diocesan bishop in the Anglican Church may have a **suffragan bishop**, **area bishop** or **assistant bishop** to assist in the task of oversight. A suffragan bishop is subordinate to a diocesan bishop and does not have a specific geographical area. (In the Catholic Church this is equivalent to an auxiliary bishop.) An area bishop has powers legally delegated to him or her and responsibility for an area within a diocese but does not have a cathedral. Assistant bishops are most often retired bishops or bishops who have returned from an overseas diocese and do not have a diocese in the Church of England. Although the Church of England has women deacons and priests, it does not currently have women bishops.

In the Catholic Church a **suffragan** bishop leads a diocese that is part of a province headed up by a metropolitan archbishop, and an **auxiliary** bishop assists in running the diocese.

Canon

In the Anglican Church this is the title given to a member of the governing body of a cathedral (the Chapter) and they can be ordained or lay. They are known as residentiary canons, and the majority exercise a ministry that is related to the life of the cathedral – its worship (see 'Precentor'), its pastoral work (canon pastor) or its teaching and educational work (canon theologian). However, some residentiary canons exercise most of their ministry in a diocesan role, e.g. as a director of ordinands or a diocesan missioner.

The ministry of senior parish clergy may be recognised by their being appointed as **honorary canons**. They receive no additional remuneration but do have a limited role in the governance of the cathedral. Lay people who have made a significant contribution to the life of a diocese may also be appointed as honorary lay canons. Canons have a designated seat in the cathedral (a stall) which they can occupy by right.

Cardinal

A senior ecclesiastical official in the Catholic Church, normally a bishop. A cardinal leads either a diocese or archdiocese or is head of a department in the Roman Curia (the central governing body of the Church). Since the tenth century, popes have been elected by the cardinals (the College of Cardinals) meeting in **conclave** – a word that derives from the tradition that the cardinals are locked (*con clave*, 'with a key') in a room until they have elected the new pope.

Churchwarden

A lay official in a parish church elected by the parishioners at an Annual Vestry Meeting. Normally there are two churchwardens in a parish, but for historical reasons in some parishes there may be more. At one time one churchwarden would be appointed by the parish priest (commonly called the rector's warden) and the other by the people (the people's warden). They are now both elected by the parishioners and hold office for a length of time agreed by the Parish Church Council, of which wardens are ex-officio members. They have responsibility for the upkeep of the church buildings and have specific powers to keep order in both the church and the churchyard. They are also responsible for keeping a record of church property and valuables. They have a duty to represent the laity and to cooperate with the parish priest (incumbent).

Curate

An ordained assistant to a parish priest. In the Church of England a curate is normally someone who has recently been ordained and who is continuing their training 'on the job' in a parish with a more experienced priest. After ordination as a deacon, a curate usually continues as a deacon for about a year and is then priested. These days it is normal for a person to remain a curate for about three years before moving on to be a parish priest (see 'Vicar', 'Rector').

Deacon

The first of the traditional three orders of ordained clergy: deacon, priest, bishop. There are some things a deacon cannot do that a priest can: preside at the Holy Communion service (they cannot consecrate the bread and the wine), give a blessing or announce the formal absolution (God's forgiveness of sin). It is not usual for a deacon to conduct a wedding service although some do. Some deacons are permanent deacons, i.e. they always serve the church in that capacity and do not become priests. More usually a deacon proceeds to the priesthood after a year or so.

Dean

This is a title given to someone who holds certain positions of responsibility within the church – the positions vary in different churches. In the Anglican Church a dean is the most senior clergy person in a cathedral (the 'mother' church of an ecclesiastical area known as a diocese) and second in seniority in the diocese to the diocesan bishop. In the past a distinction was made between a dean and a **provost**, the latter being the senior person in a cathedral that did not have an ancient foundation but had been a parish church. This distinction of title no longer exists. Westminster Abbey has a dean although it is not a cathedral but is a Royal Peculiar, i.e. it falls directly under the jurisdiction of the monarch and not a bishop. Royal Peculiars date originally from Anglo-Saxon times.

In the Scottish Episcopal Church, the senior clergy person of the cathedral is called a provost and the dean is a senior cleric who assists the bishop in the administration of the diocese.

District chairman

A senior minister in the Methodist Church, responsible for a large geographical area, e.g. East Anglia, comprising a number of circuits, or groupings, of local Methodist churches. A district is roughly comparable to a diocese in the Anglican or Roman Catholic Churches and the District Chairman has an overseer role roughly similar to that of a bishop. They hold the appointment for between five and ten years.

Elder

In a general sense an elder is someone of recognised wisdom exercising a leadership role within a church community. Depending on the denomination, they may be ordained or lay and be involved in specific areas such as administration, pastoral care, or teaching and preaching.

Minister

This can have a very wide meaning designating anyone who has a role within a church and is therefore exercising ministry. More specifically it is used in some Protestant churches to denote an ordained leader (see 'Elder' and 'Presbyter') and within free churches to denote an 'authorised' leader.

Monsignor

An honorary title given to certain priests in the Catholic Church (see also 'Canon').

Padre

The word comes from the Latin *pater*, meaning 'father', which is a common title for a priest. Padre has come to be used more specifically for priests serving as chaplains in the armed forces. Service- and ex-servicemen and women often call any priest 'Padre'.

Parson

This is an alternative name for a parish priest or clergyman. The name derives from the word 'person', the parson being the ordained 'person', the church representative, in the parish. In the Catholic Church prior to the Reformation (sixteenth century), it was the title given to the priest of a parish that did not come under the control of a monastery or other religious institution. In the Church of England it was in common use until the mid nineteenth century but has now largely been replaced by the term 'vicar'.

Pastor

Commonly used as the title of an ordained or authorised minister in churches such as Baptist churches or in Pentecostal and black-led churches. It derives from the New Testament Greek and means 'shepherd', and therefore denotes a person who is responsible for the leadership and care of a congregation. In some churches, pastors may be lay people and be those who have specific responsibility for the care of members of the congregation or community.

Pope

The title of the Bishop of Rome and head of the Catholic Church and of Vatican City. It comes from the Latin *papa* meaning 'Father', a title in the early Church for a bishop, which after the eleventh century was used exclusively by the Bishop of Rome. The authority of the Pope derives from the tradition that the Bishops of

Rome are successors to St Peter, whom Jesus described as the rock on which the Church would be founded (Matthew 16:18, 19). A further title is 'Vicar of Christ' – Christ's representative on Earth. This title too was originally used by other bishops but from the thirteenth century was exclusively used of the Bishop of Rome to denote his position over the worldwide Church and not simply over his diocese.

Precentor

The holder of this role has responsibility for organising worship in large parish churches and cathedrals. In a cathedral, a precentor is normally a residentiary canon (see 'Canon'). The title comes from the Latin meaning 'first singer' and refers to the role in the ancient Church of being the leading singer in the liturgy. The precentor was also responsible for giving the correct musical note to the bishop and the dean at the singing of the Mass. The succentor, or 'second singer', gave the note to the other clergy. Some cathedrals have retained the position of succentor, assisting the precentor.

Presbyter

The name comes from the Greek *presbuteros* and in the New Testament denotes the leader of a congregation. This led, via the Latin, to being translated as priest. In some Protestant churches the use of 'priest' for the ordained leader of a congregation has been objected to, in part because the New Testament speaks of the priesthood of all believers, and to single out ordained leaders as priests strips the laity of their priestly status. They therefore adopted either 'elder' or 'presbyter' for the ordained leader.

Priest

An ordained person, the second of the traditional three orders of ordained clergy: deacon, priest and bishop.

The term priest has long had associations with sacrifice. In many ancient religions and including the religion of the Hebrew people at the time of Abraham, this would have included human sacrifice. In the Old Testament there were priests appointed to oversee and administer the sacrifices of animals in the Temple. Rules governing the selection, practice and responsibilities of priests are set out in the book of Leviticus. Sacrifice was seen as a way of offering thanksgiving or of seeking forgiveness. Christians believe that on the cross Christ made a unique sacrificial offering of himself 'for the sins of the world' and that this has ended the need for further sacrifices.

In some churches this has led them to avoid the use of the word priest for a 'minister' or church leader so it is clear that nothing the minister does could be interpreted as a sacrifice. However, in Anglican, Catholic and Orthodox churches, for example, the term has been retained in part because of its ancient tradition but also because, especially in the Catholic and Anglo-Catholic tradition, the action of the priest at the altar during the Holy Communion service is understood to be a 're-presenting' or 're-offering' of Christ's sacrifice on the cross in the bread and the wine, the Body and Blood of Christ.

Titles of those who had positions of leadership in the early Church were somewhat fluid but by the third century the roles of bishop, priest and deacon had become more clearly established and have persisted in such churches as the Orthodox, Catholic and Anglican.

In the Catholic Church the priest who has responsibility for a parish is known as 'the parish priest' (although in America he is known as 'pastor') and any subordinate priest in the parish is known as an 'assistant priest'. In the Anglican Church the priest with responsibility for a parish normally has the title vicar or rector and junior priests are known as curates.

Reader

The Anglican Church has had readers (also known as lay readers) since 1866. Women have been licensed as lay readers since the first World War. Readers are trained lay people whose ministry includes liturgical and pastoral responsibilities. They can conduct funerals but not weddings. For services they normally wear robes similar to clergy choir robes (cassock, surplice and scarf) but the scarf is blue rather than black. Their function is similar to that of a local preacher in the Methodist Church, although local preachers have generally enjoyed a higher status than readers. Since 1972 a reader in the Catholic Church has been a recognised ministry (previously a minor order) that is open to lay people and not, as previously, only to candidates for ordination. The reader is authorised to read passages from the Bible (but not the Gospel at the Mass) and may lead intercessions, direct the singing and help instruct the faithful in the meaning and reception of the sacrament.

Rector

An ordained person who is responsible for a parish or a series of parishes. The title is ancient and originally referred to the 'owner' of a parish, e.g. a local landowner or a religious order, and means 'ruler'. If the rector were ordained he could himself be the parish priest, or if he were lay or he owned many parishes he would appoint a priest to run the parishes where he did not reside. This person was known as the vicar (see 'Vicar').

Following a ruling by King Ethelwulf in 855, the church and its priests were supported by the people of the parish who made their payment in kind, i.e. in agricultural and other produce. This was the 'tithe', meaning 'tenth'. The rector had the right to the greater tithe – corn (any cereal crop), hay, peas and beans, and wood. The lesser tithe consisted of things like wool, milk and eggs and went to the vicar. Traditionally, therefore, a rector was more important than a vicar, but although the different titles remain, the difference in status no longer exists.

Rural or area dean

In the Church of England, and many other parts of the Anglican Communion, parishes are grouped together for administrative purposes into deaneries. Traditionally these were known as **rural** deaneries but in urban areas it is more usual these days to call them **urban** or **area** deaneries. A deanery is usually led by a priest from one of the parishes in the deanery together with a lay chairperson, with whom they share chairing the meeting of the deanery synod (governing body).

Vicar

An ordained person who is responsible for a parish or a series of parishes. Originally a vicar was a deputy appointed by a rector (see 'Rector') to be the parish priest. The word 'vicar' comes from the Latin *vicarius*, meaning someone who is a representative, substitute or deputy.

When the church and its priests were supported by the payment of 'tithes' (a tenth of agricultural and other produce), the greater tithe (corn, hay, wood, peas and beans) went to the rector and the lesser tithe (things like wool, eggs and milk) went to the vicar. Although this system of payment no longer exists, the titles of rector and vicar remain. Due to the ancient distinction whereby the vicar was subordinate to the rector it is still thought, erroneously, that a parish with a rector is more important than one with a vicar.